The PayPal Official Inside

GROWING YOUR BUSINESS

Make money the easy way

Michael Miller

PayPal | Press

The PayPal Official Insider Guide to Growing Your Business
Michael Miller

This PayPal Press book is published by Peachpit.
For information on PayPal Press books, contact:

Peachpit
1249 Eighth Street
Berkeley, CA 94710
510/524-2178
510/524-2221 (fax)

Find us on the Web at: www.peachpit.com
To report errors, please send a note to errata@peachpit.com

Project Editor: Michael J. Nolan
Development Editor: Margaret Anderson/Stellarvisions
PayPal Press Editor: Matt Jones
Production Editor: David Van Ness
Copyeditor: Gretchen Dykstra
Proofreader: Jan Seymour
Indexer: Joy Dean Lee
Cover Design: Aren Howell, Charlene Charles-Will
Interior Design: Charlene Charles-Will
Compositor: David Van Ness

ISBN 13:   978-0-321-76852-0
ISBN 10:   0-321-76852-3

9 8 7 6 5 4 3 2 1

Printed and bound in the United States of America

To Sherry, as always.

Acknowledgments

AUTHOR'S ACKNOWLEDGMENTS

Thanks to my old friend Michael Nolan for thinking of me for this project, and to Margaret Anderson for shepherding it through the process. Thanks also to Matt Jones and all the folks at PayPal for providing the opportunity and helping to make this book a reality.

PAYPAL PRESS ACKNOWLEDGMENTS

PayPal Press would like to thank David Hershfield, Sarah Brody, Janet Isadore, Cynthia Robinson, Cynthia Maller, Anjali Desai, Jacqueline Cisneros, Angelo Vergara, Sumin Eng, and Sophia Cheng, among many other talented PayPal contributors, for their outstanding creative and constructive reviews. Most especially, we'd like to applaud Michael Budwig, our product manager, whose great subject-matter expertise was only matched by his superb dedication to this book's success. And for his singular focus on bringing the first PayPal Press book to print, a very special thanks to Matt Jones.

Foreword

Whether you're shopping for clothes from your computer or mobile phone, or selling artworks around the globe, you face a dizzying array of choices and decisions. How do I pay? How do I get paid? What if something goes wrong?

The answer? PayPal.

We are—and will continue to be—the leader in helping you send or receive payments, anytime and anywhere.

PayPal was founded in 1998 as the first web-native payment system. Innovation drives our business. Our Internet roots position us to expand PayPal as technology continues to change the way business gets done.

In the end, merchants and their customers want simple, safe, time-saving ways of doing business. They don't want to be bogged down with confusing choices. Whatever your idea, business, or payment need, PayPal can bring it to life, and you'll enjoy a competitive advantage that comes with ease of use.

Once you've become the expert you didn't expect to be, you'll be prepared for the next wave of innovation and change in commerce. Best of all, those changes will seem familiar because they'll be built on what you already know. After you get the basics, the rest is easy.

—Sam Shrauger
Vice President, PayPal Global
Product & Experience

Contents at a Glance

Contents

Part 1

GETTING
STARTED

1

Why PayPal?

If you've ever purchased anything online, chances are you're familiar with PayPal. PayPal is an online payment service that enables businesses of all sizes, as well as individuals, to accept bank or credit card payments for the items they sell. When a customer pays for his or her purchases, PayPal processes the payment and transfers the funds to the seller's PayPal account. PayPal also offers a start-to-finish shopping cart and checkout system.

PayPal facilitates online payments for hundreds of thousands of Internet e-commerce ventures, as well as traditional brick-and-mortar businesses that have an online presence. Read on to learn why, for many sellers, PayPal is a necessary component of doing business online.

How PayPal Works

PayPal's mission is to "build the Web's most convenient, secure, cost-effective payment solution." But what is it that PayPal does, exactly?

A Typical Transaction

Let's take a look at a typical online transaction involving PayPal, as shown in **Figure 1.1**:

1. The transaction starts when a customer (let's call her Mary Ann) goes to the website of an online clothing retailer. Mary Ann finds a sweater she wants to purchase and *clicks the Buy button* on the product page.

Figure 1.1

A typical PayPal transaction sequence.

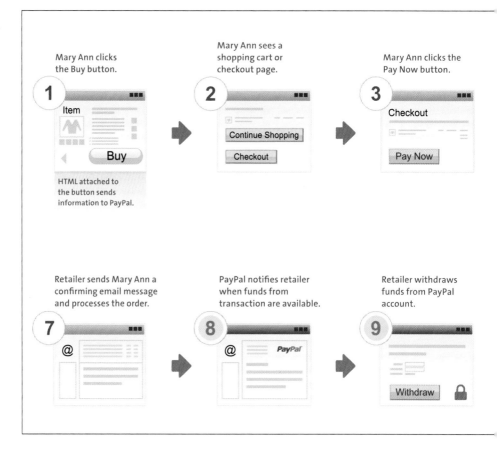

At this point, PayPal steps in behind the scenes. The retailer has followed PayPal's instructions and inserted the necessary HTML code onto the Buy button on the site's pages. When Mary Ann clicks the Buy button, an electronic command is sent over the Web to PayPal. PayPal now takes command of the rest of the purchasing process.

Mary Ann can, if she chooses, resume shopping on the merchant's website, but to keep this example simple, let's say she chooses to finalize her purchase.

2. *Mary Ann sees a shopping cart or checkout page.* Depending on the type of PayPal service involved, she might see a shopping cart page at the

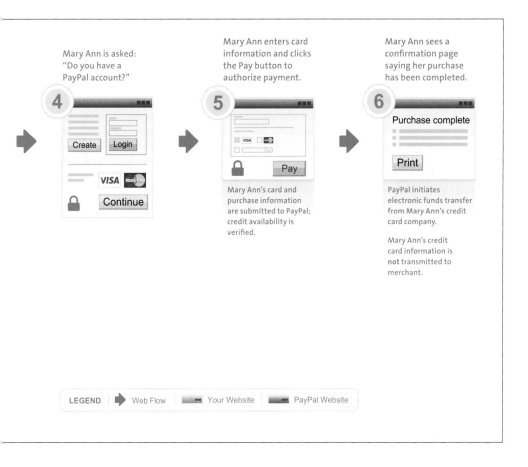

merchant site, or one that appears integrated with the merchant website. In other instances, Mary Ann will see a shopping cart or checkout page hosted at the PayPal site (labeled with the merchant's name).

In either case, the item that Mary Ann wants to purchase is listed, as well as other information such as price, shipping and handling charges, and applicable sales tax. (PayPal automatically fills in the shipping and handling charges as well as the sales tax based on the retailer's prearranged instructions.)

3. Mary Ann concurs with the total amount listed on the checkout page, so she *clicks the Pay Now button*. This directs her to a payment page, again hosted by PayPal.

4. *Mary Ann is now asked if she already has a PayPal account.* If she does, Mary Ann can simply enter her user name and password, and the rest of her personal information—address, phone number, and so on—are retrieved from PayPal's database and automatically entered onto the payment form. (And if Mary Ann doesn't yet have a PayPal account, she can now create one, if she wishes.)

5. Let us say that Mary Ann doesn't have a PayPal account—she is not forced to create one, she can simply pay using a credit or debit card. She enters her contact information and card information in the web form. *Mary Ann then clicks the Pay button to authorize payment.*

NOTE: All PayPal transactions take place on web pages that utilize Secure Sockets Layer (SSL) encryption. This protects the customer's personal data from prying electronic eyes and identity thieves.

Behind the scenes, Mary Ann's credit card information is transmitted to PayPal, which contacts the issuing bank for Mary Ann's credit card. Assuming that Mary Ann's credit line can cover the purchase, the issuing bank authorizes the transaction and the sale is charged—to PayPal.

6. *Mary Ann is sees a confirmation page with a message (sent by PayPal) that says her purchase has been completed.* Behind the scenes, the retailer is also notified by PayPal of the purchase, typically via an

email message that includes information about the purchased item, as well as Mary Ann's shipping information. At the same time, an electronic funds transfer is initiated from Mary Ann's credit card company to PayPal; the funds don't arrive immediately, but the transfer process is started.

Note what *doesn't* happen at this point: Mary Ann's credit card information is retained by PayPal, but not transmitted to the retailer. This keeps Mary Ann's financial information secure, and helps to protect her credit card number from theft.

7. Once notified of the purchase, *the retailer begins processing the order, and may send a confirmation email of its own to Mary Ann*, letting her know that the purchase has been put into its system, and notifying her of the approximate ship date. The item purchased is pulled from inventory, packed, and sent to the designated shipping service.

8. For its part, PayPal now waits for the funds to be transferred from Mary Ann's credit card account to its bank account. Once the funds are confirmed from the credit card company, *the retailer's account is credited that amount*—minus applicable fees.

9. *The retailer can now withdraw the funds from Mary Ann's purchase.* Some retailers withdraw all of their accrued funds at the end of the day or the end of the week; some withdraw funds as soon as they're available. In any case, the retailer has the option of having PayPal send it a check, or of having the funds electronically transferred to the retailer's bank account. It might take a week or more to cut and mail a check; an electronic funds transfer typically takes no more than two to three days. Or the funds can be left in the PayPal account for use in paying business expenses directly.

And, of course, Mary Ann receives (and loves) her sweater!

And that ends the transaction. PayPal received the purchase information from Mary Ann, transmitted the order to the retailer, received payment from Mary Ann's credit card company, and then paid the retailer.

Who Pays the Fees?

It's important to note that in the online payment process, the buyer pays no fees to PayPal. He or she (your customer) pays only the cost of the item purchased, plus applicable shipping and handling charges and sales tax, as determined by you, the merchant.

 NOTE: Fees are current as of May 2011, but are subject to change without notice.

As the seller, on the other hand, you pay PayPal a percentage of the total transaction amount (2.2%–2.9%, depending on the seller's monthly sales volume) plus $0.30 per transaction. PayPal pays you, the merchant, the total amount paid by the customer minus these transaction fees.

For example, let's say that Mary Ann's sweater cost $20, plus $5 shipping and handling. (We'll assume that Mary Ann doesn't have to pay sales tax, to simplify the example.) That's a total of $25 that PayPal receives from Mary Ann.

However, PayPal doesn't deposit $25 into the retailer's PayPal account. First, it deducts 2.9% of the total (73 cents) plus an additional 30-cent transaction fee. So that's $25 minus $0.73 minus $0.30, for a remainder of $23.97 that's deposited into the retailer's account. Put another way, the merchant paid $1.03 in fees to PayPal. (This is pretty close to what the

PayPal INSIDER ————————————————————

🏠 Our Business Model

PayPal is in business to serve our customers, and also to make a profit for our shareholders.

You might be surprised to learn that the fees we collect from merchants don't always generate a lot of profit. That's because we have to pay fees of our own to the credit card companies to use their processing networks when credit cards are used. These processing costs are very close to the fees that we charge our merchants.

In other words, we try to keep our fees as low as possible.

Instead, like a bank, we make most of our profits from interest on the money we handle. There's a lag between when we receive funds from the credit card companies and when those funds are withdrawn by our merchants. Even if it's only a day or two, during the time the funds reside in PayPal's corporate bank account, interest is earned on the money. Because we're handling a few million transactions a day, you can see how quickly the pennies add up. That's how we're able to offer such competitive card processing rates; we don't have to mark things up a lot.

merchant would pay a traditional credit card processing service, as you'll learn later in the book.)

Why Use PayPal?

Whether you're buying or selling online, PayPal offers some significant benefits. In fact, PayPal's benefits to both customers and merchants are hard to beat.

Benefits for Consumers

PayPal's primary benefit for consumers is that it enables them to pay for online purchases, even from smaller businesses, with a credit card. That's a big deal; without PayPal, many online merchants wouldn't be able to accept credit card payments, making it impossible for many potential customers to shop with them.

PayPal also offers consumers an unmatched level of convenience. PayPal users don't have to enter their payment and shipping information every time they buy something online; they simply log in to their PayPal account and that information is accessed automatically when they're ready to buy. It's a faster checkout process, which customers like.

It's also a more flexible checkout process, in that PayPal lets consumers choose from multiple payment methods from a single online wallet. They can store more than one credit card in a PayPal account, or opt for electronic withdrawal from a bank account, and then choose the preferred payment method when they check out from any given site.

Finally, PayPal's Purchase Protection program and its arsenal of antifraud tools safeguard consumers from unauthorized transactions as well as purchases that go bad. And since PayPal handles all of their financial information, customers don't have to worry about sharing that data with each and every e-commerce site. Their credit card numbers and bank account details are stored only with PayPal and are never shared with the merchants they buy from.

Bottom line, PayPal offers your customers availability, convenience, and security.

Benefits for Businesses

Likewise, PayPal's value proposition for businesses is arguably unmatched when it comes to payment processing services.

ACCEPTING CREDIT CARD PAYMENTS

The most obvious benefit for many businesses is that PayPal lets even the smallest merchant accept customer payments via credit card. It goes without saying that without credit cards as a payment option, your business is dead in the water. PayPal lets you compete with big operations.

SHOPPING CART AND CHECKOUT SYSTEMS

The advantage of having a ready-to-go checkout and back-end system goes without saying. It takes a lot of time and money to build your own online checkout system; many smaller and mid-sized merchants simply can't do it. Again, this is where PayPal shines—you get a checkout system that looks like it's part of your site, but actually is run by PayPal.

CONVENIENCE

The ability to accept credit payments and offer a ready-made checkout system speaks to another benefit—convenience. You don't have to go to multiple suppliers to offer these features on your site; PayPal is a one-stop shop for all the payment functions you need. And, as you'll learn throughout this book, PayPal makes it easy to set up any and all of these options; there's not a lot of complicated programming necessary, even for some of the more sophisticated functions.

EASE OF REGISTRATION

Speaking of easy, let's talk for a moment about signing up for PayPal's services—as compared to applying for a traditional merchant credit card account. PayPal's registration for a business account is pretty much a one-page fill-in-the-blank process; upon approval, you're up and running (and accepting credit card payments) in no time.

Contrast that with the process of applying for a merchant account with most credit card processors, which involves reams of forms, credit checks, and providing more information than most merchants are comfortable with. And, even after all this hassle, you might not qualify for an account—or qualify only at a higher rate. Many online ventures are simply too small to qualify for a merchant credit card account, period.

NOTE: If you wish to add Website Payments Pro to your account, you do need to apply and be vetted, which can take a day or two.

SECURITY AND FRAUD PROTECTION

You want to run your online business without fear of online fraud and theft. Once again, PayPal comes through, offering superb security and fraud protection for both consumers and merchants, including buyer address confirmation. Many accounts, especially those for smaller businesses, include a comprehensive seller protection program. You don't have to worry about fraudulent transactions while using PayPal; PayPal is a strong line of defense for merchants of all sizes.

PCI COMPLIANCE

Have you ever heard of something called the Payment Card Industry Data Security Standard, or PCI DSS? It's a set of requirements set forth to ensure that all companies that process, store, or transmit credit card data maintain a secure environment. Essentially, PCI DSS is a security standard designed to make sure that consumer credit card data is not compromised.

If you have a merchant credit card account, you're required to become PCI compliant which includes completing an annual self assessment and quarterly system scans. Jumping through those hoops costs time and money. (You pay for the system scans.)

However, if you use PayPal solutions like Website Payments Standard or Express Checkout for all of your credit card processing, you don't have to worry about complying with the PCI standard. That's because you never see your customers' credit card data; your customers transmit their credit card information directly to PayPal. So you don't have to take the time or spend the money to become PCI compliant—and your customers are ensured a safer transaction experience.

(The exception to this is if you handle your own credit card data and use PayPal only for payment authorization via Website Payments Pro or Virtual Terminal. In this instance, you still need to ensure your own PCI compliance, as customers' credit card data passes through your hands.)

REDUCED COSTS

Of particular importance to many businesses, PayPal may reduce your overall payment processing costs. Merchants that use PayPal find that they have fewer chargebacks, less fraud, and fewer customer complaints than they do with traditional credit card processing services.

For that matter, the whole PayPal checkout process tends to reduce a merchant's customer service requirements; it's an easier and less problematic process, as well as one that many customers are already familiar with. Put simply, PayPal takes a lot of the pain out of payment processing—for both customers and merchants.

INCREASED LEGITIMACY

It's also worth noting that displaying the PayPal logo can add legitimacy to your online business—especially if you're a newer or smaller business. You may not have the name recognition of larger online merchants, but with the PayPal logo displayed on your checkout pages, customers know they can trust you. And that may mean the difference between making or losing a sale.

ACCEPT INTERNATIONAL TRANSACTIONS

The more places you can sell your products and services, the more sales you'll make. To that end, PayPal makes it easy for you to accept payments from international customers. (In fact, PayPal's international payments are fairly transparent to the merchant.) If you can handle shipments outside the U.S., PayPal can handle non-U.S. payments in most major currencies—including currency conversion. It's remarkably easy, and can significantly expand the scope of your business.

INCREASED SALES

Adding international sales can increase your sales, but that isn't the only way PayPal works to expand your business. PayPal can bring you new customers and help you make more money from your existing customers.

Research shows that online merchants that offer PayPal as a payment option reach a wider audience than non-PayPal sites. A 2010 PayPal survey found that small- to medium-sized businesses that offered PayPal Express Checkout in addition to traditional credit card payments registered an 18 percent average increase in sales.* Over 80 percent of those merchants surveyed reported some sort of sales increase from the PayPal option, and the increase typically started within two months of implementation. The increase, by the way, was incremental, and did not take away from existing credit card volume.

In addition, PayPal users tend to shop more frequently and spend more online than do non-PayPal users. Suffice it to say, when you tap into the PayPal user base, you'll benefit.

Bottom line, implementing PayPal payments on your site can bring you new customers and increase the conversion from existing customers, driving incremental sales. You can't ignore that.

MORE SATISFIED CUSTOMERS

Those new customers you get from PayPal, as well as your existing customers who pay via PayPal, are more satisfied customers. PayPal inspires customer confidence and is in fact easier to use than most other checkout systems, which means a more pleasant experience for your customers. Easier purchasing means more satisfied purchasers—which is always good for your bottom line.

Paying for PayPal

We've talked a little bit about fees throughout this chapter, but let's explore that in more detail, beyond our typical example.

As noted previously, PayPal charges no fees to buyers; the merchant pays all the fees for a given transaction. There are two kinds of fees charged: a percentage of the total transaction amount and a fixed per-transaction fee.

As of March 2011 PayPal's percentage transaction fees range from 2.2% to 2.9%, depending on your monthly sales volume. Add a flat $0.30 fee per transaction and you have the total fee.

---

* Independent survey by Ipsos Public Affairs of 805 PayPal Merchants, July 2010, where an average 18 percent increase in sales was reported since adding PayPal Express Checkout.

Table 1.1 presents PayPal's fee schedule as of May 2011 (subject to change, of course):

Table 1.1 PayPal Merchant Fees (U.S.)

Monthly Sales	Transaction Fee
$0–$3,000.00	2.9% + $0.30
$3,000.01–$10,000.00	2.5% + $0.30
$10,000.01–$100,000.00	2.2% + $0.30

This table only presents transaction fees as of May 2011; depending on the tools you use other fees may apply, such as the $30 per month fee for Website Payments Pro.

PayPal's transaction fees are based on the *amount of money transferred*. This point is important. PayPal charges fees based on the total amount of money paid, *not* on the selling price of the item. That means if a $10 item has a $5 shipping and handling cost, the customer pays a total of $15— and PayPal bases its fee on that $15 payment. So you need to factor your PayPal fees on the total of item price plus shipping and handling costs.

PayPal INSIDER

 ### Simplifying the Fees You Pay

PayPal's fees are fairly simple. Depending on your monthly sales volume, we charge between 2.2% and 2.9% of the total transaction, plus $0.30 per transaction. It doesn't matter what payment method the customer uses, or who the customer is: your fees are the same.

That's not the case with traditional merchant credit card processing services. Fee structures can be very complex. If consumers use special 'vanity' cards, for example, you (the merchant) pay a higher fee, without the consumer's knowledge. There are many variables, which makes planning difficult and reporting cumbersome.

At PayPal, we prefer to take that complexity out of the equation for our merchant customers. We charge you the same rate no matter which card a customer is using. The 2.9% (or lower) rate applies to all purchases.

This is important to keep in mind when comparing rates between PayPal and other services. In addition to setup fees, fixed monthly fees, and terminal/software fees, you should compare the transaction fees charged, and whether they are variable.

> ⚠️ **CAUTION:** When comparing fees with traditional merchant credit card processors, make sure you include *all* fees charged—including fees for renting a terminal, leasing processing software, and the like.

Finding Out More—and Getting Help—on the PayPal Site

This chapter only scratches the surface of what PayPal offers to online merchants. When you want to learn more, it's best to go directly to www.paypal.com, PayPal's website. Click the Business tab, shown in **Figure 1.2**, and you'll see all sorts of links that will help you learn more about what PayPal is, how it works, and how it can help your business.

Figure 1.2

Learn more about PayPal's business services online.

In addition, the PayPal site offers a robust help system for both consumers and merchants. Just click the Help link at the top of any page to browse a broad list of support topics, or use the Search box to look for answers to specific questions. You'll also find a link to PayPal's Community Help forum, where you can get assistance from other PayPal users, as well as a link to query an automated service rep online. There's a lot of help available—if you need it!

The Bottom Line

PayPal is one of the world's largest online payment services, providing credit card processing and other transaction services for individuals and businesses worldwide. Businesses use PayPal not only to process credit card payments, but also to provide the entire online transaction process, including shopping cart and checkout services. PayPal offers merchants a high level of service, as well as the possibility for increased sales, at competitive rates—and with fewer and simpler fees than typical traditional merchant credit card processing services.

2

Choosing the Product that Fits

PayPal offers a variety of products for businesses of every size and type—everything from simple Buy Now buttons to complete shopping cart and checkout systems. And it's more than just an online payment method; PayPal also offers back-office tools to handle accounts payable, accounts receivable, inventory, and the like.

With all these options available, how do you decide which PayPal products are right for your business? Does Web Payments Standard provide what you need, or do you need to get Web Payment Pro? What is Express Checkout and what advantages does it offer? Read on to find out.

What Kind of Merchant Are You?

Every merchant is unique. A small business selling comic books online has very different needs than a large general merchandise retailer selling online as an adjunct to traditional direct mail sales. Even within a particular category, competitors often approach the marketplace from distinct perspectives, and thus have different payment processing needs.

Because of this, there's no such thing as a one-size-fits-all payment processing system. That's why PayPal offers a variety of products designed with different types of merchants in mind.

All of this begs the question: What type of merchant are you? Your individual requirements will dictate which of PayPal's solutions are best for you.

Small and Focused

The Internet has been a boon for small and focused retailers in many product categories. Whether you're selling clothing, collectibles, or car parts, you have a limited number of items but still hope to generate significant revenues from online sales. You don't necessarily need to build a custom shopping cart or checkout system, but you do need to get your business online as quickly and as easily as possible.

In fact, you don't even have to be a business, at least in the traditional sense of the word. Many individuals sell merchandise on their websites, either goods that they produce themselves or items they're reselling from other sites or retailers. When you're an individual selling on your own website, you need a simple payment processing solution that lets your customers click a button to initiate a sale and that lets you accept credit cards with a minimum investment of time or money. PayPal's answer is Website Payments Standard, which we'll discuss in short order.

Broad Selection

The Internet is also home to many merchants who offer larger selections of merchandise. We're not talking about a dozen or a hundred products, but rather thousands of SKUs sold through a large and sophisticated e-commerce website.

If you're a broad-based e-commerce enterprise, chances are you already have a shopping cart and checkout system in place. Maybe you've contracted with a third-party shopping cart service, or maybe you have a custom-designed cart and checkout. Whatever the case, you still have payment processing needs, and are looking for a solution that will integrate into your current setup.

For this type of seller, PayPal offers Website Payments Pro. As you'll learn shortly, this is a more sophisticated solution than Website Payments Standard, and it's better suited for merchants who process a large number of items through an existing checkout system.

Big and Getting Bigger

The biggest merchants already have their systems set up, and already have established accounts for credit card processing. That's true even for traditional brick-and-mortar businesses (like catalog and direct mail retailers) that are just now moving online; the systems already exist, even if e-commerce functionality is relatively new.

If you have payment processing in place and don't want to abandon your current systems and suppliers, the best solution is Payflow Payment Gateway, where payment information flows through PayPal to an established processor. You add online payments to your existing services, with the benefit of PayPal's reporting and fraud protection. Even better, you can accept payments from PayPal customers outside of traditional credit card transactions. It's a solution for the biggest players, proving that PayPal has something for merchants of every size and type.

Examining PayPal Products

All told, PayPal offers six key payment processing solutions: Website Payments Standard, Website Payments Pro, Payflow Payment Gateway, Express Checkout, Virtual Terminal, or Online Invoicing. As you might suspect, these solutions are tailored for different types of businesses, and each has its own specific features and fees.

Table 2.1 compares these various products; we'll look at each one in more detail, as well.

Table 2.1 PayPal Payment Products

Product	Setup Fee	Monthly Fee	Transaction Fee	Features
Website Payments Standard	None	None	2.2%–2.9% + $0.30	Easy setup Payment buttons PayPal Shopping Cart Transaction pages hosted on PayPal
Website Payments Pro	None	$30.00	2.2%–2.9% + $0.30	Integrates with existing shopping carts Direct Payment for credit/debit cards Express Checkout for PayPal payments Transaction pages hosted on your website
Payflow Link Gateway	$179.00	$19.95	$0.10	Integrates with existing merchant account First 500 transactions free Transaction pages hosted by PayPal
Payflow Pro Gateway	$249.00	$59.95	$0.10	Integrates with existing merchant account First 1,000 transactions free Transaction pages hosted on your website
Express Checkout	None	None	2.2%–2.9% + $0.30	Express Checkout Adds PayPal payments to existing checkout system (customers must have PayPal accounts)
Virtual Terminal	None	$30.00	2.4%–3.1% + $0.30	Enables phone and mail payments No hardware or software required
Online Invoicing	None	None	2.2%–2.9% + $0.30	Email customer invoices Add PayPal button to QuickBooks/Quicken invoices

NOTE: All fees discussed in this chapter are current as of May 2011, but are subject to change without notice. Fees stated are for domestic transactions, in U.S. dollars; these fees may be different if you use different currencies.

Website Payments Standard

Website Payments Standard is the easiest way to add PayPal payments to your website. All you need is a rudimentary knowledge of HTML to add some simple PayPal payment buttons to your web pages; customer checkout is processed on the PayPal site. There is no setup fee for this service and no ongoing monthly fees; all you pay are the normal PayPal transaction fees.

Many businesses choose PayPal's Website Payments Standard because adding it doesn't require a lot of programming skill, and there's no need to create a custom checkout service. Adding PayPal payment for an item is as simple as choosing a payment button for the item, generating the code for that button (which PayPal does), and then copying and pasting that code into your web page.

In other words, Website Payments Standard provides you with payment buttons for items on your website, as well as a PayPal-based shopping cart and checkout system. It's a total back-end solution for merchants of any size.

HOW WEBSITE PAYMENTS STANDARD WORKS

With Website Payments Standard, when a customer clicks the PayPal payment button, she's taken to the checkout system on the PayPal website. You can customize, to some degree, the checkout page that the customer sees, but PayPal handles the entire checkout process. The customer arranges payment on this checkout page and then is returned to a designated page on your site.

At the same time, PayPal notifies you of the purchase, typically via email. You can then print a packing slip or shipping label directly from your PayPal account overview page, or otherwise process the order and arrange shipping through your own systems.

PAYPAL SHOPPING CART

Part and parcel of the Website Payments Standard is the PayPal Shopping Cart. This is ideal for merchants who do not yet have their own shopping cart systems; when you use the PayPal Shopping Cart, you don't have to purchase or develop your own custom shopping cart.

The PayPal Shopping Cart operates like any third-party shopping cart system. Customers can add multiple items to their cart while shopping, and then check out to purchase all items in a single transaction. Purchasing an item is as simple as clicking the Add to Cart button.

Customers can view the contents of the shopping cart at any time by clicking the View Cart button, placed strategically on your product pages. From there they can also conclude their shopping and pay for their purchases, via a checkout page on the PayPal site, as shown in **Figure 2.1**. The payment process is handled completely by PayPal and includes all forms of credit card payment.

FEES

Website Payments Standard is not only easy to integrate, it's also easy to pay for. There are no initial setup fees and no monthly fees. You pay only the standard transaction fees due when a customer buys something from you.

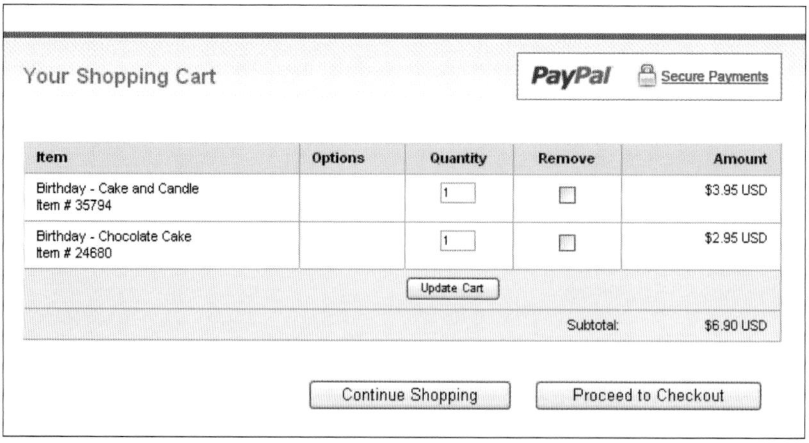

Figure 2.1

A typical checkout page generated as part of the PayPal Shopping Cart.

Item	Options	Quantity	Remove	Amount
Birthday - Cake and Candle Item # 35794		1	☐	$3.95 USD
Birthday - Chocolate Cake Item # 24680		1	☐	$2.95 USD
		Update Cart		
			Subtotal:	$6.90 USD

Your Shopping Cart — PayPal — Secure Payments

Continue Shopping   Proceed to Checkout

Website Payments Pro

Website Payments Standard is a great solution for many merchants, but it does rely on PayPal for the shopping cart and checkout process—during this process, it transfers your customers to the PayPal site. If you'd rather host your own shopping cart and checkout system on your website, you can opt for Website Payments Pro.

Website Payments Pro provides both a merchant account and a processing gateway to retailers who have an established shopping cart system. Because of this, it isn't quite as easy to implement as Website Payments Standard. Indeed, implementing Website Payments Pro requires more extensive programming knowledge, as you have to tie your site into the PayPal site using the PayPal Application Programming Interface (API). This process isn't for the fainthearted or the technically inexperienced; most businesspeople turn this task over to a tech expert.

HOW WEBSITE PAYMENTS PRO WORKS

Website Payments Pro lets you accept payments via credit card, debit card, or PayPal account directly on your website. This requires the implementation of two separate but related payment solutions:

- **Direct Payment** enables you to accept both credit and debit card payments directly from your site. Customers pay for their purchases within your checkout system, and the payments are processed by PayPal.

- **Express Checkout** enables you to accept payments from users with PayPal accounts. Customers click the Checkout with PayPal button and are then prompted to enter their PayPal account information. (Obviously, this is a faster way for PayPal customers to check out—even when paying by credit card—as they don't have to reenter their shipping and billing information.)

NOTE: Payments made via Direct Payment are not covered by the PayPal Seller Protection Policy. Learn more about PayPal's seller protection in Chapter 11, "Dealing with Disputes and Chargebacks."

Figure 2.2
How Direct Payment and Express Check-out work.

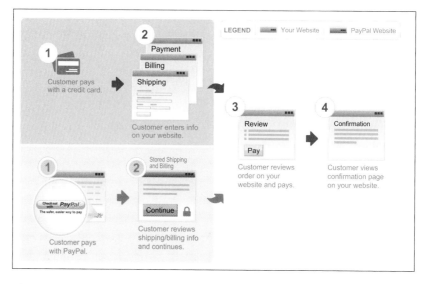

This dual option of credit/debit card and PayPal payments is becoming increasingly common. **Figure 2.2** shows the relationship between Direct Payment and Express Checkout to a buyer.

Both of these payment solutions are implemented by calling the appropriate PayPal API operations, which means doing the necessary programming on your website.

ADDITIONAL FEATURES

Website Payments Pro includes a number of other tools in addition to the payment processing features. These include

- **Recurring billing**, for automatic billing of subscriptions and other recurring transactions. (This option costs $30/month in addition to the regular Website Payments Pro fees.)

- **Virtual Terminal**, for accepting phone, fax, and mail payments.

- **International transactions**, which lets you accept payments in six major currencies: U.S. dollars, Australian dollars, Canadian dollars, GB pounds, Japanese yen, and euros. PayPal also offers automatic currency conversion (for an additional fee).

- **Shipping tools**, to collect shipping address information, and print packing slips and shipping labels with prepaid postage.

- **Reports**, including account activity summary, monthly sales, transaction details, and the like.

- **Seller Protection Policy**, which covers eligible Express Checkout transactions against unauthorized payments, item-not-received claims, chargebacks, and reversals. (This is not available for Direct Payment transactions.)

- **Automatic fraud screening**, complete with address and card verification checks, as well as 128-bit SSL encryption.

- **Advanced fraud management filters**, up to 17 in total, that let you target specific threats to your business. These are in addition to PayPal's basic fraud management filters, of course—and are available for an additional fee.

FEES

Because of its technical complexity, Website Payments Pro is more costly to use than Website Payments Standard. While there are no setup fees or contracts to sign, you do have to pay PayPal a set $30/month usage fee, in addition to the normal per-transaction fees.

Payflow Payment Gateway

The Payflow Payment Gateway is designed for larger retailers who have their own merchant accounts. It's particularly useful for traditional brick-and-mortar businesses who want to add e-commerce to their mix. This service connects your site to any major credit card processor or bank, and adds PayPal as an auxiliary payment option. You use the Payflow Payment Gateway to help build your checkout system and manage all your customer payments—PayPal and otherwise.

Figure 2.3
How the Payflow Payment Gateway works.

HOW THE PAYFLOW PAYMENT GATEWAY WORKS

A payment gateway is a secure connection from your online store to your existing Internet merchant account and payment processing network. **Figure 2.3** shows how the process works.

As such, PayPal's Payflow Payment Gateway is ideal for merchants who want to manage their own customer payments (except credit card processing, of course) and keep their customers on their own sites throughout the entire checkout process. You use your own checkout system and existing merchant account to accept customer payments; payment information is sent via the gateway to PayPal for additional processing, transaction reporting, and other services.

You can also add Express Checkout to Payflow to process transactions from PayPal users. That's a nice addition to standard credit and debit card payments.

There are actually two different Payflow services available:

- **Payflow Link**, which is a more basic service with easier setup. It enables your customers to complete their transactions on customizable pages hosted by PayPal.

- **Payflow Pro**, which is the full-blown, fully customizable gateway service. It enables customers to complete their transactions securely on your website.

Both solutions let you accept credit cards, debit cards, and (with the Express Checkout option) payments from PayPal accounts. Both solutions also offer 128-bit SSL encryption, and integrate with most third-party shopping carts.

NOTE: Implementing the Payflow Gateway requires a bit of programming and working with a variety of PayPal APIs. To that end, PayPal offers a Payflow Software Developers Kit (SDK) to help smooth the process. More details are available at www.x.com, PayPal's website that provides support and instruction for developers and application programmers.

ADDITIONAL FEATURES

The Payflow Payment Gateway offers many of the same services found in Website Payments Pro. These features include

- Recurring billing
- Virtual Terminal
- International transactions
- Reports
- Automatic fraud screening
- Fraud management filters

FEES

As befits its unique nature, the costs for using the Payflow Gateway are also somewhat unique. You pay a one-time setup fee, a flat monthly usage fee, and then $0.10 per transaction. (Your first 500 or 1,000 transactions are free, however.) Unlike the Website Payments products, there is no percentage transaction fee charged. **Table 2.2** details the costs for both Payflow Link and Payflow Pro.

Table 2.2 Payflow Gateway Pricing

Gateway	Setup Fee	Monthly Fee	Free Monthly Transactions	Price per Additional Transaction
Payflow Link	$179.00	$19.95	500	$0.10
Payflow Pro	$249.00	$59.95	1,000	$0.10

Express Checkout

If you already have a website with a merchant account and a checkout system set up, you can use PayPal's Express Checkout (sometimes called the Additional Payment Option) to add PayPal payments to your website. This is a great way to expand your customer base to those who prefer to pay with their PayPal accounts. You still accept credit and debit card payments as usual, but offer the Checkout with PayPal option for a more streamlined—and much quicker—checkout experience.

Naturally, for all transactions completed via Express Checkout, you can take advantage of the associated PayPal services—reports, fraud protection, seller protection, international currency support, and the like. Setting it up requires a minimal amount of programming to call the appropriate PayPal APIs; it's also preintegrated with a number of third-party shopping cart solutions.

There is no setup fee to use this service, nor are any monthly fees charged. All you pay are PayPal's normal per-transaction fees.

Virtual Terminal

If you have an existing direct mail or phone-based business, or wish to add phone or mail sales to your online store, look at PayPal's Virtual Terminal. It's essentially an online version of a traditional credit card swipe machine, so you can process all those phone, fax, and mail orders via your existing computer system.

PayPal INSIDER

 Why Virtual Terminal Transactions Cost More

You may be wondering why the transaction fees for Virtual Terminal transactions are higher than those for online sales. It's all about risk. It's because direct mail and phone purchases have a higher incidence of both fraud and chargebacks. That's partly due to the nature of these sales, where the customer is not present.

The rates we charge for virtual transactions like these are very competitive with what you'll find from other payment processing services. When making your comparisons, pay particular attention to the setup costs; we don't require any special software, as many other services do.

With Virtual Terminal, you don't have to purchase or rent any new hardware, nor install any new software; it's all web-based, which means you can use it on any computer or mobile device that is connected to the Internet. To process an order, just log into the Virtual Terminal application on the PayPal website, enter the details of the order (including credit card information), and you're done. PayPal handles all the processing and transfers the appropriate funds into your PayPal account.

PayPal's Virtual Terminal is an affordable alternative to those old-fashioned (and expensive) swipe machines. There is no setup charge, and you pay a $30/month usage fee. (This fee is waived if you use Virtual Terminal along with Website Payments Pro.) Transaction fees run from 2.4% to 3.1%, depending on your monthly sales volume, plus $0.30 per transaction. (Table 2.3 details these fees.)

Table 2.3 Virtual Terminal Fees

Monthly Sales	Transaction Fee
$0 to $3,000	3.1% + $0.30
$3,000 to $10,000	2.7% + $0.30
$10,000+	2.4% + $0.30

Online Invoicing

PayPal's email payments solution, dubbed Online Invoicing, enables you to email invoices to your customers and then accept secure online payments. It's ideal for business-to-business companies, or for online retailers who bill their customers on a regular basis for products or services sold.

The process is pretty much what you'd expect. You create an invoice via PayPal, or add a PayPal button to invoices created in QuickBooks or Quicken. The invoice is then sent to the customer via email. When the customer receives the invoice, she can pay (via PayPal) by clicking the appropriate button or link within the email invoice. Payment can be via a PayPal account, bank account, or credit card, all processed by PayPal. When the payment is processed, PayPal notifies you and transfers the funds into your PayPal account.

Best of all, there are no setup or monthly fees associated with this product. You pay only the normal PayPal transaction fees.

Choosing the Right PayPal Option for Your Business

As you can see, PayPal offers a variety of payment solutions to meet the needs of its varied merchant customer base. With so many options, it can be a little challenging to decide which product is the best for any given business.

Which, then, is the right one for you? Let's start by walking through the checklist in Table 2.4; determine which items are most important to you, and then see which PayPal options address that item.

What does all this mean, in practical terms? Here are some concrete recommendations:

- If you're an individual or a smaller merchant selling online, with a limited number of SKUs, go with **Website Payments Standard**. This solution is easy to implement, with little to no technical skill required, and provides you with a free shopping cart.

PayPal INSIDER

 A Matter of Size

Which option you choose depends largely upon the size of your business.

We've found that most small- and medium-sized businesses select Website Payments Standard. It's an easy solution to implement without technical expertise and an all-in-one solution—you don't have to build or buy your own checkout system. With this approach you rely on the checkout pages at PayPal.

For larger merchants who already have a shopping cart/checkout process in place, the most popular solution is Website Payments Pro. You use your checkout system and keep customers on your site, and let us do the payment processing.

Among even larger merchants that already have established merchant credit accounts, or traditional retailers just now moving online, many prefer the Payflow Pro solution.

- If you're a new merchant who hasn't yet decided on a shopping cart, **Website Payments Standard** provides you with a free shopping cart. If your needs are more sophisticated, look for a third-party shopping cart provider that supports **Website Payments Pro**.

- If you're an established online merchant with an existing shopping cart, go with **Website Payments Pro** with the **Express Checkout** option.

Table 2.4 PayPal Decision Checklist

	Website Payments Standard	Website Payments Pro	Payflow Link	Payflow Pro	Express Checkout	Virtual Terminal	Online Invoicing
Want to accept credit/debit cards payments	●	●	●	●		●	●
Want to accept PayPal payments	●	●	●	●	●	●	●
Need shopping cart/checkout	●						●
Already have third-party or custom shopping cart/checkout		●	●	●	●		
Want to keep customers on your website for all processing		●		●			
Already have merchant credit card account			●	●			
Want to add PayPal payments to existing credit card processing					●		
Want to accept phone, fax, and mail orders						●	
Want to send customer invoices via email							●
Don't have access to advanced programming	●					●	●
Credit application required		●	●	●			

This lets you take advantage of PayPal processing for all your credit card orders while maintaining your existing checkout process, and offers the benefit of accepting PayPal payments in addition to credit cards.

- If you're a traditional merchant just now adding an e-commerce functionality, chances are you already have a merchant credit card account and are happy with it. What you need is the ability to accept payments online, which you get with **Payflow Pro**. Add **Express Checkout** to enable customers to pay via PayPal accounts, too.

- If you invoice a significant percentage of your customers, go with **Online Invoicing** in addition to any other services you may need.

- If you accept telephone or fax orders, add **Virtual Terminal** to any other services you may subscribe to.

Obviously, there are exceptions to every recommendation and every business is different, but this advice will get you started. If you're still not sure which solution is best for you, then give us a call at 1-888-818-3928. Our sales associates will be glad to answer all your questions and help you choose the product that best serves your business needs.

Signing Up for PayPal

Now that you know which PayPal solutions are best for you, it's time to sign up. That means creating a PayPal account and choosing which services to use.

Establishing a PayPal Account

Before you can use any of PayPal's business solutions, you need a PayPal account. PayPal offers three account types, only one of which is appropriate for businesses.

If you've ever purchased anything via PayPal or on eBay, you've probably created a **PayPal Personal** account. This type of account is designed primarily for individuals who shop online.

If you've ever sold anything on eBay, you're likely to have a **PayPal Premier** account. This type of account is designed for individuals selling online—primarily but not exclusively on eBay. A Premier account enables individuals to accept credit card payments, but doesn't offer many features of value to larger businesses.

The type of account your business needs is appropriately named the **PayPal Business** account. It's tailored specifically for online merchants, and lets you choose from a variety of different payment products.

So if you haven't yet established a PayPal Business account for your company or organization, now's the time to do it. (Or, if you already have a Personal or Premier account, now's the time to upgrade to a Business account.) Creating an account is part of the process of choosing a PayPal payment solution; you'll be prompted for the necessary information as you go through the process.

Preparing to Sign Up

Just what information do you need to sign up for PayPal? Here's what you should prepare:

- Business type (individual, sole proprietorship, partnership, corporation, nonprofit organization, or government entity)
- Business name
- Business address, city, state, and ZIP code
- Business phone
- Business category (arts, crafts, and collectibles; baby; beauty and fragrances; books and magazines; business-to-business; clothing, accessories, and shoes; computers, accessories, and services; education; electronics and telecom; entertainment and media; financial services and products; food retail and service; gifts and flowers; government; health and personal care; home and garden; nonprofit; pets and animals; religion and spirituality (for profit); retail (not otherwise classified); services—other; sports and outdoors; toys and hobbies; travel; vehicle sales; and vehicle service and accessories)

- Business subcategory (specific to the chosen major category)

- Average transaction price, for transactions through PayPal (less than $25; $25–$50; $50–$100; $100–$250; $250–$500; $500–$1,000; $1,000–$2,000; $2,000–$5,000; $5,000–$10,000; more than $10,000)

- Average monthly sales volume, through PayPal (less than $5,000; $5,000–$25,000; $25,000–$50,000; $50,000–$100,000; $100,000–$250,000; $250,000–$500,000; $500,000–$1,000,000; more than $1,000,000)

- Sales venues (where you do business—eBay, other online marketplace, your own website, or other)

- Percentage of annual revenue from online sales (less than 25%, 25%–50%, 50%–75%, or 75%–100%)

- Date your business was established (month and year)

- Your customer service email and phone number

- The name, address, and phone number of the primary business contact

- Your email address and desired password (at least 8 characters with a mix of uppercase and lowercase letters, numbers, and symbols), along with the typical password recovery questions

- A credit application, required for Website Payments Pro and other advanced solutions. (PayPal will check your credit history as part of the application process for these services.) As of 2011–12 an SSN or EIN will be required, to comply with a new IRS regulation.

Getting Started

To sign up for your PayPal Business account and choose a payment solution, follow these steps:

1. Go to the PayPal home page (www.paypal.com).

2. Click the Sign Up link at the top of the page.

Figure 2.4
Getting ready to sign up for a Business account.

3. When the Create Your PayPal Account page appears, as shown in **Figure 2.4**, select the appropriate country and language (United States and English by default), and then click the Get Started button in the Business section.

4. When the Select Payment Solution page appears, as shown in **Figure 2.5**, pull down the list and select a payment option (Website Payments Standard, Website Payments Pro, Virtual Terminal, PayPal as an Additional Payment Option, Email Payments, PayPal for Your eBay Business, or Payflow Gateway), and then click the Continue button.

5. When the first Business Account Setup page appears, as shown in **Figure 2.6** (on the next page), provide the information requested, and then click the Continue button.

Figure 2.5
Choosing a PayPal payment solution.

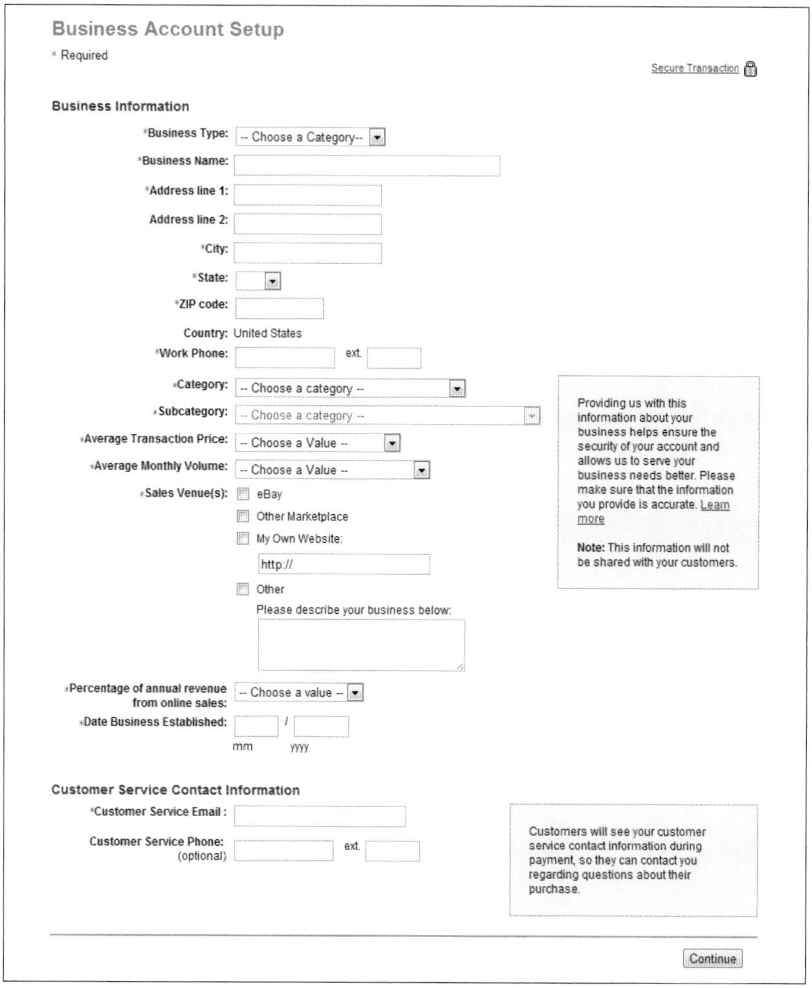

Figure 2.6
Entering key information about your business.

6. When the second Business Account Setup page appears, provide the information requested, and then click the Continue button.

What happens next depends on the solution you've selected. Follow the onscreen instructions to complete your application and start implementing the services you need.

TIP: You're not locked into the service you initially sign up for. If you need additional features, you can upgrade to a higher level of service at any time.

The Bottom Line

PayPal offers a variety of payment solutions, each tailored to specific business needs. For most smaller and mid-sized merchants, Website Payments Standard provides a complete start-to-end system, including a shopping cart and checkout system. For businesses that already have a checkout system, Website Payments Pro lets you integrate that system with PayPal payment processing. For merchants that already have a merchant credit account and want to take advantage of PayPal's processing and reporting, PayPal offers the Payflow Payment Gateway. And Express Checkout service adds a PayPal payment as an option to credit card processing. In addition, PayPal offers a Virtual Terminal for phone and mail payments, as well as an Online Invoicing solution for billing customers via email. Most businesses will be able to find the right combination of features among these many payment options.

NOTE: PayPal also offers a variety of payment solutions for mobile commerce. Find out more in Chapter 15, "Mobile and PayPal." For more detailed information on PayPal's mobile solutions, look for the companion book from PayPal Press, *The PayPal Official Insider Guide to Mobile Profits*, available at bookstores everywhere.

3

Integrating PayPal with Your Site

You've evaluated the options and decided to use PayPal for online payment processing. Perhaps you want to integrate PayPal into your existing e-commerce website. Or, you might be an established retailer but new to online selling. Or perhaps you're launching a completely new venture.

You've determined which of the many PayPal products is best for your business. Now it's time to implement PayPal on your website. Read on to learn how to integrate the PayPal features you need with those offered on your existing site—or, if you're starting from scratch, how to build a new site with PayPal in mind.

Integration Options

When it comes to integrating PayPal features with your website, there are several approaches you can take, each associated with specific PayPal offerings. As you might suspect, some of these approaches are easier to execute than others.

In general, integration means inserting some sort of code into the underlying code of your existing website. Some of this code inserts things like buttons and links necessary for your customers to purchase items and access their shopping cart and checkout system. Other code links information on your site, and input by your customers, to functionality hosted by PayPal. Still other code generates forms to accept customer information or even checkout pages. Which and how much code you need to insert depends on the PayPal products you choose.

If this all sounds a bit technical, it is. If you know your way around HTML, great. If you're more of a businessperson than a developer, that's okay, too; you can always arrange for a developer to do the coding for you. In fact, you really don't need to handle any of the technical details—just choose the PayPal solutions you want and let the technical folks handle the integration.

HTML Integration

The simplest type of PayPal integration involves the use of blocks of HTML code. HTML integration can be undertaken by anyone with a basic familiarity with HTML coding. In the simplest forms of integration, PayPal generates the actual code—all you have to do is insert it into the appropriate page on your site.

There are two PayPal solutions you can implement via simple HTML coding:

- **Website Payments Standard**. With this option, favored by many smaller retailers, PayPal services are integrated with your website or e-commerce application via HTML code. The simplest approach is to create payment buttons using PayPal's button creation tool; you can create Buy Now, Add to Cart, View Cart, Subscribe, and Donation buttons that link to the proprietary PayPal Shopping Cart. You can also use HTML code to link these buttons to third-party shopping carts and checkout systems.

NOTE: Learn more about these and other PayPal payment options in Chapter 2, "Choosing the Product that Fits."

- **Payflow Link**. This HTML-based product provides a gateway between your shopping cart and your merchant services account. Payflow Link gives you secure order pages, hosted at PayPal, that you can customize.

Whichever solution you choose, HTML integration is pretty much a one-time setup. You go to the PayPal site to generate the HTML code for the elements you need, and then insert that code into your web pages. You only have to update or add new code if you change the products or features you offer on your site.

PayPal's HTML-based solutions are simple to implement because all the back-end operations take place on the PayPal site. As you can see in Figure 3.1, you don't host the shopping cart or checkout system, and thus don't have to generate shopping cart and checkout pages. Instead, clicking a Purchase or Payment button takes customers to PayPal's site, where all the heavy lifting takes place. (Customers are returned to your site at the end of the process.)

1 Buyer checks out.

Buy Now

2 PayPal processes payment.

I Agree

Continue

3 Buyer returns to your website.

Confirmation

Figure 3.1
PayPal's HTML-based checkout process; customers are directed to PayPal's site for completion.

NOTE: The transfer to PayPal's site is seamless and can be invisible, depending on how you configure your checkout pages on PayPal's site.

Let's say you're an individual who's offering a single product for sale, something like a self-published book or manual. You can easily create a page on your website to promote this book and add the requisite PayPal payment button. For that matter, you can insert a payment button on your site's home page, or even in the sidebar of your blog. It's a one-time thing; insert the code and forget it. PayPal will handle all subsequent orders and notify you when there's been a purchase and you need to ship your product.

When a customer clicks the Buy Now button, he's taken to the checkout system on PayPal's site, where the transaction is completed. It's not an entirely customized solution, in that it isn't as branded as it would be if you built your own checkout system. However, as an individual or small retailer, you get a ready-made payment processing system with minimal effort (and zero upfront cost) on your part. However, if you have a larger variety of products, or if your offerings change frequently, it can be tedious to keep updating the bits of code on your site.

API Integration

If you do not want to use PayPal's hosted checkout, then you must make use of their APIs to integrate PayPal features into your website. These APIs link data from your website to the PayPal system in real time, thus providing a constant connection between your site and PayPal. Unless you're using a third-party shopping cart, this adds another level of complexity.

PayPal INSIDER

 ### HTML Integration, the Best Option for Smaller Sellers

If you're a small business or individual offering only a few products for sale online, we recommend PayPal's Website Payments Standard. It's easy to add a payment button to your website or blog by inserting a few lines of HTML code; PayPal handles the shopping cart and checkout processing. There's no need to build or buy your own shopping cart or checkout system.

As you can see in **Figure 3.2**, PayPal's API-based solutions keep customers on your website throughout the checkout process; the APIs "talk" to PayPal to obtain necessary information or perform required functions. PayPal does the payment processing, and then sends the resulting information back to your site (or to a third-party checkout system, if that's what you're using) for completion and display.

If you've developed and are hosting your own shopping cart and checkout pages, the API programming is more involved than simply inserting a few lines of HTML code into a web page. The API functions must be incorporated within the code or script that retrieves information from the customer, sends that information to PayPal, calls the appropriate PayPal function, and then returns the processing information back to your website for display and further use. As such, API programming is not for the technically inexperienced; you'll need a qualified developer to do the appropriate programming on your website.

NOTE: API stands for Application Programming Interface. An API is a set of rules or specifications that a web or software developer can work with to access and make use of services and resources provided by another website or software program. In essence, an API acts as an interface between different web pages or software programs.

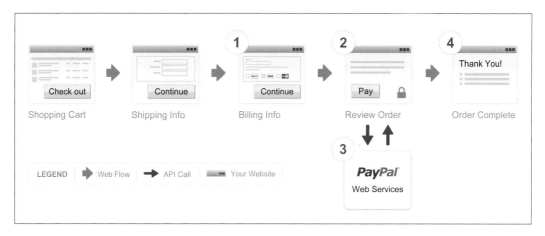

Figure 3.2 *PayPal's API-based checkout process; customer and product data is transferred to PayPal and back again for completion.*

PayPal products that utilize API integration include

- **Website Payments Pro**, an all-in-one payment solution that functions as both a merchant account and a payment gateway.

- **Payflow Pro**, which uses PayPal APIs to provide a payment gateway between your existing merchant credit card account and PayPal, so you can process credit card transactions online.

- **Express Checkout**, which is typically used with another PayPal service (such as Website Payments Pro and Payflow Pro) and gives users with PayPal accounts a streamlined experience.

ADVANTAGES OF THE API-BASED APPROACH

The HTML button solution is great for small or occasional sellers. But if you have more products for sale, the many buttons that were each added by hand become a challenge to maintain. Also, you might decide that you don't want to send all of your paying customers to the PayPal site for order completion. It's better to keep them on your site (for generating additional orders) and in a fully customized and branded environment.

With any of PayPal's API-based options, you (or your developer of choice) must do a bit more programming, as you have to build your own check-out pages and integrate a custom or third-party shopping cart solution. But using PayPal's APIs lets you keep the customer on your site, with only the customer's payment and shipping information flying back and forth to PayPal for processing. The customer stays on the branded check-out page you designed and is still on your site in case he wants to buy anything else.

In terms of cost, PayPal's API solutions cost no more than the HTML solutions—zero, in terms of PayPal charges. (You still pay for each transaction, of course.) You will incur greater development charges to build your own shopping cart and checkout system, but that's the cost of creating a fully functional, fully customized solution for your site.

Obviously, if you're running a big box-sized business, it's worth the expense to build a branded checkout solution; you wouldn't want to rely solely on PayPal Buy Now buttons and send all your customers to PayPal to pay.

THIRD PARTY SHOPPING CARTS

Let's not forget that API integration exists for most major third-party shopping carts. If a shopping cart offers integration with PayPal, chances are it's done via APIs—but you don't have to deal with all the programming. This is a popular choice for many mid-sized businesses.

There might be PayPal-specific configuration settings for the cart, but if the product is any good they should walk you through what's needed. If you have unusual needs the cart might accommodate a bit of custom scripting, but in general there should not be any coding required. It's a great way to get what looks like a custom solution with a minimal amount of technical investment—and look like you're a big operation.

Implementing the Integration

If you've decided on HTML buttons or homegrown API-based payment solutions, how do you integrate it into your website? There's a bit of work involved, no matter which approach you select.

Examining the Process

Implementing PayPal processing is a multistep process. Here's what you and your developer need to do:

1. Select the best product for your business.

2. For HTML-based solutions, generate the code for the buttons you wish to use, *or* for API-based solutions, obtain the code necessary to call the appropriate APIs from your website.

3. Insert the necessary code into the appropriate pages on your website.

4. Test the integration, using the PayPal Sandbox testing environment (or third party shopping cart site).

5. Based on the test results, update your integration configuration as necessary.

6. Go live with your updated web pages.

> **NOTE:** If you've chosen a third-party shopping cart, you'll need to read the documentation for that product with respect to integrating PayPal.

Who Does the Work?

All of that sounds simple enough. But who does all the work?

It depends.

Again, if you're already using a third-party shopping cart service that offers PayPal integration, you may not have any work to do. For many merchants, this is probably the easiest way to go.

If you're implementing a relatively simple HTML-based solution (a few payment buttons, let's say) and you're somewhat technically adept, then you may be able to do the work yourself. Implementing this type of solution involves generating a snippet of HTML code and then inserting that code on your web page where you want the payment button to appear. If you're comfortable with doing a little behind-the-scenes HTML work, then by all means feel free to tackle the project on your own.

How easy is an HTML-based solution to implement? Adding PayPal payment for an item can be as simple as inserting the HTML <form> code for a payment button.

PayPal INSIDER

 Playing in the Sandbox

One of the most popular developer tools is the PayPal Sandbox, a testing environment that duplicates PayPal's live site, but without registering real transactions. In essence, the Sandbox lets you use "play money" to test your implementation of PayPal's various HTML buttons and API calls before your site goes live. You can use the Sandbox to test the following:

- Buy Now buttons
- Subscribe buttons
- Donate buttons
- Shopping Cart buttons

- Refunds
- Payment Data Transfer
- Instant Payment Notifications
- Simulated transactions

To test in the Sandbox, you must first establish a PayPal Developer Central account. You can then create multiple test accounts for buyers and merchants, so you can simulate different scenarios to be sure everything functions as expected before launch. Go to developer.paypal.com to access the Sandbox.

The full code looks something like this example:

```
<form action="https://www.paypal.com/cgi-bin/webscr" method="post">
<input type="hidden" name="cmd" value="_s-xclick">
<input type="hidden" name="hosted_button_id" value="value">
<input type="image" src="https://www.paypal.com/en_US/i/btn/
 btn_buynowCC_LG.gif" border="0" name="submit" alt="PayPal - The
 safer, easier way to pay online!">
<img alt="" border="0" src="https://www.paypal.com/en_US/i/scr/
 pixel.gif" width="1" height="1">
</form>
```

If this code makes basic sense to you, and you know where to insert it into your website HTML, and how to get it live on your site, then you're good to go. Remember, PayPal generates the exact code you need to insert; you don't need to write it.

If, on the other hand, looking at this HTML makes your head turn, or if you simply don't have the time to do it yourself, then you'll need to pass the job off to a developer. Implementing an HTML-based integration is fairly easy for an experienced developer, and shouldn't take much time; it's something you can budget lightly for (unless you have many buttons!).

If you already have shopping cart and checkout pages on your site, it's probably not a major project for an experienced developer to connect with PayPal using their API. This is especially true if you find one that is familiar with PayPal. Remember, you don't want an amateur touching the code of your critical business functions, so leave it to a professional!

However, if you want to build a custom API-based solution for your site, that requires a lot more development time and effort. You'll need in-house IT staff or an outside developer, and you can expect a new custom system to be a longer and more involved (and thus more costly) project.

Finding a Developer—or a Shopping Cart

If you need a developer to help you with your PayPal integration, or you need to add a shopping cart to your site or even build an online store from scratch, PayPal can help. Search the PayPal Partner Directory to find developers in your area who can deliver the solutions you need.

The PayPal Partner directory lists developers and other businesses that offer all manner of PayPal-related products and services. Some PayPal partners provide prepackaged shopping cart, checkout, and storefront solutions; others can develop customized options for your business.

To access the Partner Directory, go to www.paypal.com and under the Business tab click the Partners subtab. On the Partner Program screen you'll see the Find a Partner button. When the Partner Directory page appears, as shown in **Figure 3.3**, you can scroll through the featured partners or filter the list by solutions offered or industries served. Click the link for any given partner to learn more about services offered, and then contact that developer.

Figure 3.3
*Finding a developer
in the PayPal Partner
Directory.*

Getting Help from PayPal

If you're using in-house staff to implement your PayPal integration, they're going to need documentation, API calls, and other assistance to get the job done. All of that information—and more—is available on the PayPal Developer Network website (www.x.com), shown in **Figure 3.4**.

To get full use of the PayPal Developer Network site, you'll want to formally register—although you can access much of the available information as an unregistered guest. Once you've registered, you can use the site to determine the best solution for your business, generate HTML code for payment buttons and the like, download powerful developer tools, access documentation for PayPal's various APIs, view video demos, interact with other developers and PayPal staff in online forums, and utilize a bevy of other resources.

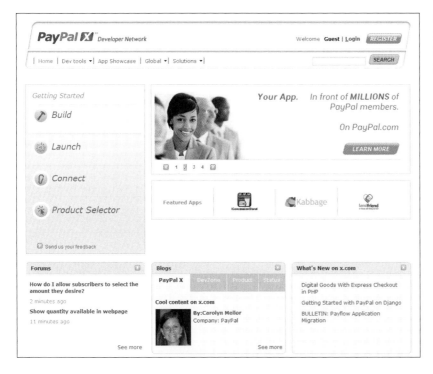

Figure 3.4
The PayPal Developer Network website.

Much useful information can be found in the various product-specific developer's guides available for reading or downloading from the website. Select Dev Tools > Documentation from the menu bar to display a list of available documentation; most of the guides can be viewed or downloaded in either HTML or PDF format. These are essential reading for anyone doing the actual work of implementing a PayPal solution.

Example 1: HTML Integration with Payment Buttons

We've talked a bit about PayPal integration in general terms. But let's look at a few examples, so you'll get a better feel for what's involved.

Our first example deals with the easiest method of integration: using the HTML-based Web Payments Standard to insert payment buttons on your website. These buttons send your customer to PayPal's website to complete the transaction; checkout does not happen at your site. You generate the necessary HTML code for each button using PayPal's Button Creation Tool.

Generating the Button Code

Before you implement this particular solution, you want to open a PayPal Business account, as discussed in Chapter 2, "Choosing the Product that Fits." With said account established, follow these steps:

1. Log onto the PayPal website (www.paypal.com).

2. Select the Merchant Services tab.

3. When the next page appears, as shown in **Figure 3.5**, click the Buy Now Button link.

4. When the Create PayPal Payment Button page appears, as shown in **Figure 3.6**, pull down the Choose Button Type list and select Buy Now. (You can also create Shopping Cart, Donations, Gift Certificates, Subscriptions, Automatic Billing, and Installment Plan buttons.)

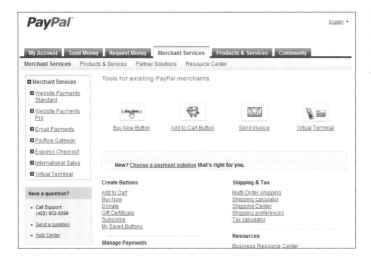

Figure 3.5
*Getting ready to
create a PayPal
payment button.*

Figure 3.6
*Fill in the form
to generate the
button code.*

5. Enter the name of the item you're selling into the Item Name box; if the item has a product number, enter that into the optional Item ID box.

6. Enter the selling price of the item into the Price box; pull down the Currency list to select a currency other than U.S. dollars (USD).

7. Customize the button, if desired (as described below).

8. Choose shipping specifics. Generally, you will check Use Settings Saved in Your PayPal profile and enter the shipping weight of the item and its packaging. To charge a different amount for shipping, check the Use Specific Amount option and enter that amount.

NOTE: Learn more about PayPal's shipping options in Chapter 7, "Shipping Orders."

9. If you charge sales tax, enter the amount of tax into the Use Tax Rate box.

10. You can link sales to your PayPal merchant account using either your Secure Merchant Account ID or your email address.

11. Click the Create Button button.

12. PayPal generates the HTML code for this button, as shown in **Figure 3.7**. Click the Select Code button, copy the code, and then paste the code into your web page's underlying code where you want the button to appear.

Figure 3.7
The HTML code for a PayPal Buy Now button.

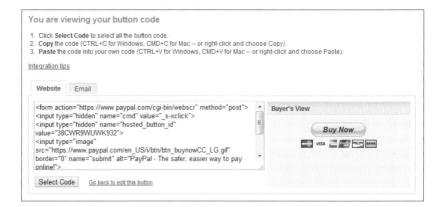

As you can see, this process is relatively simple; all you need is basic information about the item you're selling and it's easy to generate the button code. Of course, you'll need someone with a certain level of technical expertise to paste the button code onto your website, but it doesn't get much simpler than this.

Customizing the Button

You don't have to settle for the basic button. There are all sorts of customization you can add. For example, if you sell an item that has multiple variations, each at a different price, you can create a button with a pull-down options list, like the one in **Figure 3.8**; just select the Add Drop-Down Menu with Price/Option option within the Customize Button box. The customer selects which version he wants from the list, and that information is sent to PayPal along with the order.

Likewise, if you sell an item in multiple colors or sizes, all at the same price, select the Add Drop-Down Menu option. This creates a pull-down menu with the size or color options you specify, as shown in **Figure 3.9**.

You can also select options regarding the button's text and appearance. You can display a smaller button, hide the various credit card logos, change the text to another language, or have the button say Pay Now instead of Buy Now. You can even use your own button image, instead of the standard orange PayPal button. It's your choice.

Figure 3.8 *A button with pull-down option/pricing list.*

Figure 3.9 *A button with a pull-down size list.*

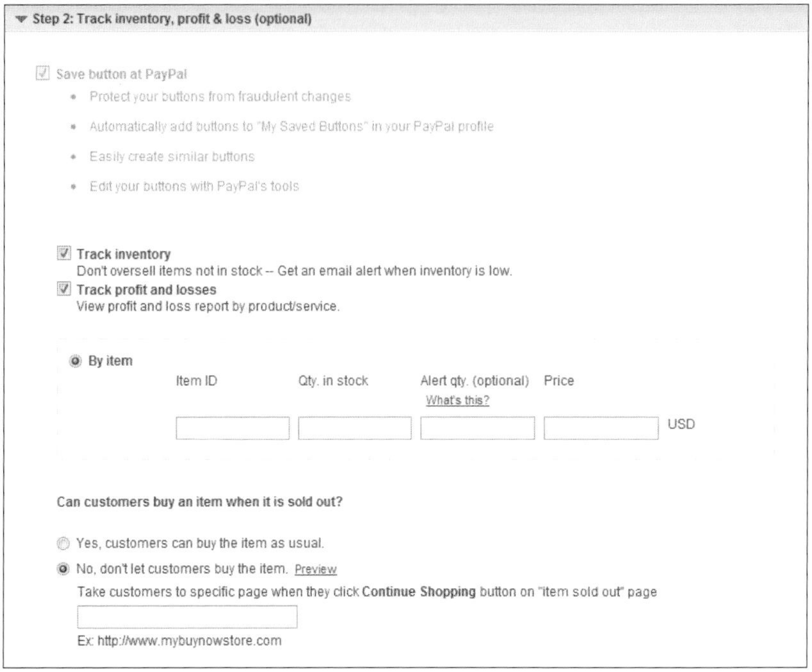

Figure 3.10

Configuring PayPal to track inventory and profit/loss of an item.

You can also have PayPal track your inventory of the item associated with this button, as well as the running profit or loss for that item. Expand Step 2 on the Create PayPal Payment Button page, shown in **Figure 3.10**, and enter the appropriate inventory and cost information; PayPal will do all the tracking and calculating when an item is sold.

Additional options are available when you display the Step 3 section of the Create PayPal Payment Button page, shown in **Figure 3.11**. You can select any or all of the following options for the customer's checkout page:

- Let the customer change order quantities.

- Let the customer add special instructions.

- Require the customer's shipping address, or not.

- Direct customers to a specific URL on your site after checkout is completed or cancelled.

As you can see in **Figure 3.11**, there's a lot you can customize—if you want.

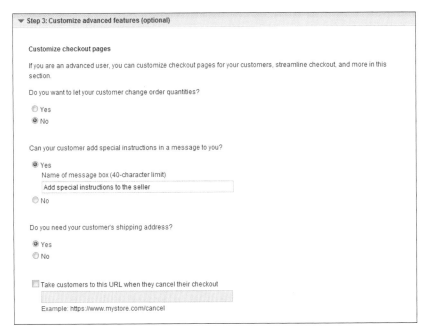

Figure 3.11
Configuring advanced options for the checkout page.

Example 2: API Integration with Express Checkout

Creating HTML-based payment buttons does not make sense if you have already developed shopping cart and checkout pages on your website. Remember, to add PayPal to your existing system will require working with PayPal's API.

As this is a book for businesses, not developers, we won't go into the nitty gritty of API programming. Instead, we'll leave you with a sense of what's involved in implementing PayPal's API-based Express Checkout solution (as an example). In general, here's what your developer will be doing:

1. Place the code for the PayPal Express Checkout button in your site's checkout flow.

2. Modify the page's underlying code to handle the button click for each button you insert, using the PayPal Express Checkout API operation to set up the interaction with PayPal and redirect the user's web browser to PayPal to initiate buyer approval for the payment.

3. Write code on your site's order confirmation page to obtain the payment authorization from PayPal and use PayPal Express Checkout API operations to obtain the customer's shipping address and accept the payment.

4. Test the integration using the PayPal Sandbox.

5. Make the pages live.

As you can see, there's quite a bit for a developer to do when you use this method, and it's all custom to your specific site and checkout system. Your developer can learn more about the necessary code at the PayPal Developer Network website (www.x.com).

The Bottom Line

There are three ways to integrate PayPal payment processing with your website. If you want to keep it really simple, you can use Web Payments Standard and HTML coding to insert payment buttons on your site. The customer is then sent to PayPal's site to complete the transaction. Remember, PayPal provides the code for you!

Alternatively, you can take advantage of one of the many third-party shopping cart products that integrate with PayPal (using either Website Payments Standard or Website Payments Pro).

Finally, you can integrate Website Payments Pro with your new or existing e-commerce system. This approach sends customer information to PayPal for payment processing, but then sends the resulting information back to your website or checkout system (custom or third party product) for finalization. This gives you more control over the checkout process overall but requires some developer time to be sure everything is coded correctly and tested.

Part 2

MANAGING
YOUR MONEY
AND YOUR
BUSINESS

4

Getting Paid

Part and parcel of the online shopping experience is the shopping cart and checkout system, which is how customers pay and you get paid. There's also the matter of invoicing your customers, if that's the way your business works, or managing recurring payments—subscriptions or installment payments.

If you don't yet have a shopping cart for your website, PayPal can provide one, at no additional charge and with little effort on your part. Otherwise, you can integrate PayPal's payment processing into your existing shopping cart—including those provided by third-party suppliers.

How Shopping Carts Work

If you offer more than just a single item for sale, chances are some customers will purchase more than one item, which is a good thing. Since you don't want to force these customers to make two or more separate payment transactions, you need to consolidate multiple purchases into a single shopping cart. That shopping cart then feeds into a checkout page, where customers provide shipping information and pay for their purchases.

The Checkout Process

Most online shoppers are familiar with shopping carts and the online checkout process. **Figure 4.1** shows how the process works, from the customer's viewpoint, using the PayPal Shopping Cart with Website Payments Standard. Steps in blue are generated pages hosted on the PayPal site; steps in white take place on the merchant's site.

The process starts when the customer clicks the Add to Cart button for a particular product. This button is hosted on the merchant's website, although it's generated via code supplied by PayPal. This adds the item to the virtual shopping cart, hosted by PayPal; customers can continue shopping—and add more items to the shopping cart—or go directly to the checkout page.

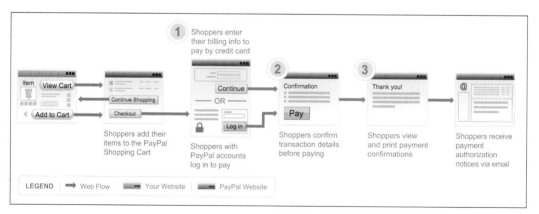

Figure 4.1 *The three steps of the PayPal Shopping Cart checkout process, in the context of an online shopping experience.*

When the customer clicks to checkout, they will see the checkout page hosted by PayPal, although it can be branded for the merchant. At this point the customer signs in and pays with a PayPal account, or enters the necessary credit or debit card information. When paying via credit or debit card, the customer also has to enter a shipping address and other relevant information. (These details are already known if the customer pays via a PayPal account.)

The shopper confirms the transaction details and then PayPal processes the payment. Assuming the customer's payment is approved, PayPal generates a confirmation screen and transmits information about the purchase to the merchant. The customer is then returned to the merchant's website, and receives (from PayPal) an email confirmation of the purchase.

Behind the Scenes

Most shopping cart/checkout systems are built from the following components:

- Payment buttons or links that enable the customer to place individual items into the shopping cart.

- A database that stores information about the products in the customer's shopping cart.

- Web pages that display information about shopping cart contents, as well as checkout pages that are used when the customer is ready to pay.

- Controls for administering the shopping cart system.

- Reports that detail shopping cart transactions.

These components work together to provide a unified shopping and payment experience for the customer, allow you to access and manage your inventory, and provide you with information that triggers the shipment of purchased products. The system itself is actually a software application. This application can run on the computer or server that hosts your company's website, or it can run on a third-party website. In the case of the PayPal Shopping Cart, it runs on PayPal's servers.

Wherever it's hosted, the shopping cart integrates with the rest of your website. When a customer clicks the Buy Now or Add to Cart button, that information is transmitted to the shopping cart. When the customer opts to check out, all items in the basket are displayed on a dynamically generated checkout page. The customer then enters appropriate payment and shipping information, the payment is processed, and the transaction is concluded—all in the shopping cart/checkout system.

The product and customer information is stored temporarily in the shopping cart database. The shopping cart system creates the final checkout on the fly, in real time, based on the information stored in the database; unlike the static HTML product pages on your website, all checkout pages are dynamic web pages.

Integrating a Shopping Cart

If you're using a third-party shopping cart, this software needs to be tied into your existing storefront and inventory systems. This requires some degree of programming expertise; how much programming is necessary depends on the complexity of the shopping cart.

For example, PayPal's Website Payments Standard provides the fully featured PayPal Shopping Cart. With this solution, all you have to do is insert HTML code for the individual product payments buttons; the checkout process itself resides on the PayPal site, so you don't have to create new pages for checkout or other activities. The integration process is relatively easy.

If you use another shopping cart solution, however, the integration process can be more complicated. PayPal's Website Payments Pro integrates with most third-party shopping carts, but may require additional programming to implement the necessary calls to various PayPal APIs.

That said, many third-party shopping carts come with PayPal integration built-in, which makes it easy for you. Some shopping cart providers build in integration with Website Payments Pro; others (those that provide their own merchant credit account solutions) use the gateway approach and tie into PayPal's Payflow Payment Gateway. In either instance, integrating PayPal with a third-party shopping cart is often as easy as providing your PayPal credentials to the shopping cart service and checking a few options on a sign-up form.

Do You Need a Shopping Cart Partner?

When it comes to implementing a shopping cart on your site, you have several options. You can

- **Build your own shopping cart from scratch**. This is expensive and time consuming, but it provides you with a totally customized solution that exactly matches the look and feel of the rest of your website. Plus, with your own shopping cart, there are no ongoing monthly or usage fees—although you'll still have to pay PayPal or another firm for payment processing.

- **Partner with a third-party shopping cart service**. These services offer ready-to-run shopping cart/checkout systems that can be somewhat customized in look and feel to match the rest of your website. Integration with your site is less costly and time consuming than building your own system from scratch, although some programming is still necessary. (The integration of the shopping cart with PayPal, however, is typically seamless; it's integrating the cart with your site that takes a bit of effort.) You'll pay a set monthly fee for the use of the shopping cart, a fee per transaction or one based on your transaction volume, and payment processing fees.

- **Use the PayPal Shopping Cart**. This is the easiest solution to implement. All you have to do is generate and insert Add to Shopping Cart button codes for each SKU on your site; PayPal handles everything else. There's no integration programming necessary (beyond the button codes, of course), and no additional programming needed on your site. You don't even have to pay for this service; the PayPal Shopping Cart has no setup fees and no ongoing monthly fees. (You do have to pay PayPal's normal payment processing fees, of course.) The primary downsides are that you send visitors away from your site for the checkout process and that PayPal's checkout pages aren't as specific to your brand or company as custom-built checkout pages.

Where do you go to implement each of these solutions? It depends on which choices you make.

Building It Yourself

If you want to build it yourself, you'll need to contract with a website development firm—typically the same folks building the rest of your site. Make sure you're dealing with a firm that has experience building e-commerce sites and systems.

 ## Content Management Systems

Most small to medium-sized online businesses do fine with a static website and shopping cart system. But if you have hundreds or thousands of SKUs, you may be better off with a more sophisticated content management system (CMS) and product database. This type of system doesn't rely on static product web pages; instead, all product information is stored in a large database, and product pages are generated dynamically when a customer browses to or searches for a particular SKU. You enter information about each product into the database, and that information is then fed into a template used for each product page.

From the customer's viewpoint, a CMS-based site looks identical to a site based on static product pages. The only visible difference is the page URL, which is short and static on a normal site, but is dynamically generated on a CMS site and can be long.

From the merchant's perspective, a CMS-based site is much more difficult to implement, at least initially. It requires quite a bit of initial coding, as well as the creation of a product database. However, many sites on the web are moving to a CMS approach with the popularity of PHP-based open source systems such as Drupal and Joomla,

which makes maintaining *all* pages at your site easier. For e-commerce specifically, ongoing maintenance is lower, as you can add new products (and new product pages) simply by adding more information to the database. Changing the price value in the database means the new price is automatically reflected in all dynamically generated product pages.

In terms of integrating with a shopping cart, there's not much difference between a traditional or CMS-based system. In a traditional system, product and pricing details are hard-coded into the product's payment button; in a CMS system, this information is pulled from the underlying database. But the checkout system works in pretty much the same way in either case, dynamically generating the checkout page and initiating the payment process.

Should you consider a content management system for your e-commerce site? Absolutely. If the learning curve, technology, and setup are too much for you, then you might decide against it, but the rewards will be considerable.

Fortunately, PayPal's Website Payments Pro and Payflow Payment Gateway solutions both integrate well with CMS-based shopping carts.

Finding a Shopping Cart Partner

If you want to go with a third-party shopping cart, there are many firms you can partner with—hundreds of them, in fact. Make sure that the shopping cart you choose integrates with PayPal, of course; in fact, many third-party shopping carts come with PayPal functionality built in.

More specifically, you need to make sure the shopping cart integrates with the PayPal product you've chosen for your business; you still need to choose between Website Payments Standard, Website Payments Pro, and the other services. Once you've ensured this compatibility, it's a matter of selecting the features, functionality, and price that work best for you.

Where can you find a shopping cart partner? PayPal maintains a list of compatible shopping carts in their Partner Directory. Go to the Solution Types pane and check Shopping Cart; PayPal now displays dozens of shopping cart providers, as you can see in **Figure 4.2**. You can sort the results by distance, company name, or PayPal partner level (Platinum, Gold, or Member.) Click through to learn more and contact any given company.

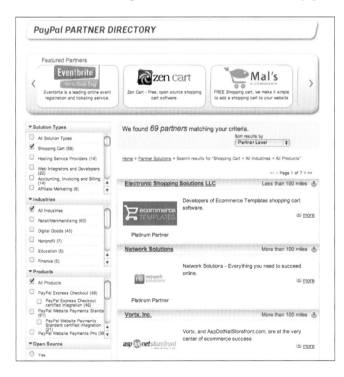

Figure 4.2

Browsing for shopping cart partners in the PayPal Partner Directory.

Selecting the PayPal Shopping Cart

The PayPal Shopping Cart is available with Website Payments Standard. When you sign up for your PayPal account, this is the solution you want to choose.

Once you've signed up, integrating the PayPal Shopping Cart into your site is a simple matter of generating HTML code for an Add to Cart button for each SKU on your site, and then inserting that code into each product page. (**Figure 4.3** shows typical results.) You'll also want to generate code for and insert View Cart buttons, so that your customers can check out and pay when they're ready.

Once all the buttons are generated and inserted, and you take your new product pages live, your shopping cart is also live. Since all the processing occurs on PayPal's site, your setup work is now done; any customer who makes a purchase will use the PayPal Shopping Cart.

NOTE: Learn more about creating payment buttons in Chapter 3, "Integrating PayPal with Your Site."

Figure 4.3
PayPal Add to Cart buttons on a typical product page.

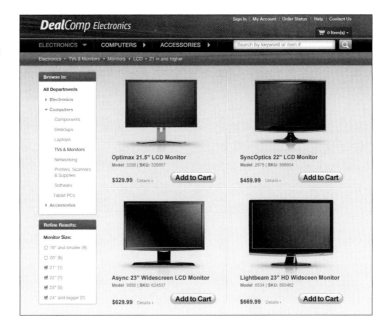

Configuring the PayPal Shopping Cart

When it comes to implementing the PayPal Shopping Cart, there are several payment options you need to configure, such as tax rate, shipping charges, and the like. While you can specify some of these settings on an SKU-specific basis when you create the product's Add to Cart button, most settings are applied universally to your entire shopping cart.

You configure these universal payment settings under the Selling Online heading of your profile, shown in **Figure 4.4**. To open this page, log in to your PayPal account, select the Profile subtab on the My Account tab and, on the left, select My Selling Tools.

NOTE: Take some time to become familiar with the choices available under the My Account tab, Profile subtab. In the future this text will simply refer to "your profile"—which, of course, you must be logged in to view.

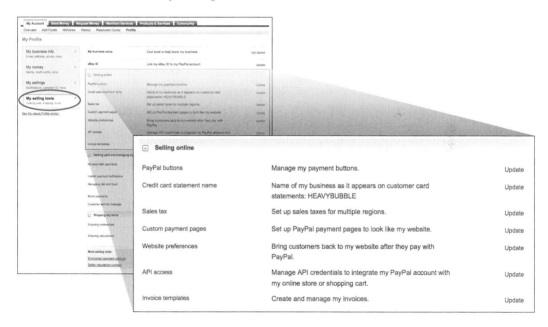

Figure 4.4 *Your PayPal profile with My Selling Tools selected on the left. This is where you configure your account's payment settings, under the Selling Online heading, by clicking to update the default settings.*

Figuring Taxes

As an online business, you may or may not be required to charge sales tax on the items you sell; it depends largely on what kind of traditional retail presence you have, and where. If you have to charge tax, go to your profile, click My Selling Tools on the left and then, under the Selling Online heading, update Sales Tax settings.

This displays the Sales Tax page, shown in **Figure 4.5**. Go to the Set Up Domestic Sales Tax Rates section and click the Add New Sales Tax link. When the Domestic Sales Tax page appears, as shown in **Figure 4.6**, select a state and enter the applicable tax rate for that state; if you need to apply sales tax for a specific city or county, click the Zip Code link and enter the ZIP code,

Figure 4.5
Getting ready to configure sales tax settings.

Figure 4.6
Specifying sales tax by state.

instead. By default, the sales tax is applied only to the product price; if tax must be applied to the entire purchase price, including shipping, check the Apply Rate to Shipping Amount box.

In most instances, you charge sales tax only for those states in which you have a physical presence. If you have a physical presence in multiple states, you'll have to specify tax rates for each state in which you do business. Click the Create Another button to add another state to your list. When you're done specifying tax rates, click the Continue button.

> **TIP:** If sales tax is different for a specific SKU, you can set a product-specific tax rate when you're creating that item's Add to Cart button. Just enter the applicable tax rate into the Tax box when you create the button.

Determining Shipping and Handling Fees

You also set universal shipping and handling fees from the same area in your profile. Click the Set Up Shipping Calculations link under the Selling Preferences heading; this displays the Shipping Calculations page, shown in **Figure 4.7**. From here, click the Start button in the Set Up Domestic Shipping Methods section. (To set up shipping fees for shipments outside the U.S., click the Start button in the Set Up International Shipping Methods section.)

What follows is a somewhat detailed process, only because you can be very specific about the shipping services you use and the fees you charge your customers. In essence, you can set shipping fees dependent on where the item is being shipped, the shipping service used, and either the item weight or price.

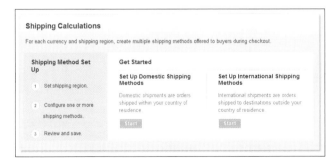

Figure 4.7

Getting ready to set shipping and handling fees.

Start by specifying where you ship to on the Shipping Region page shown in **Figure 4.8**. Click Continue and you see the Set Up Domestic Shipping Methods page shown in **Figure 4.9**. Here you select a shipping method, set your standard delivery time, determine how your rates are based (on total order amount, total order weight, or total item quantity), and then set your shipping rates, either by dollar amount or percentage. You can create multiple shipping fee schedules, for multiple shipping methods; just click the Create Another button. Click Continue when you're done.

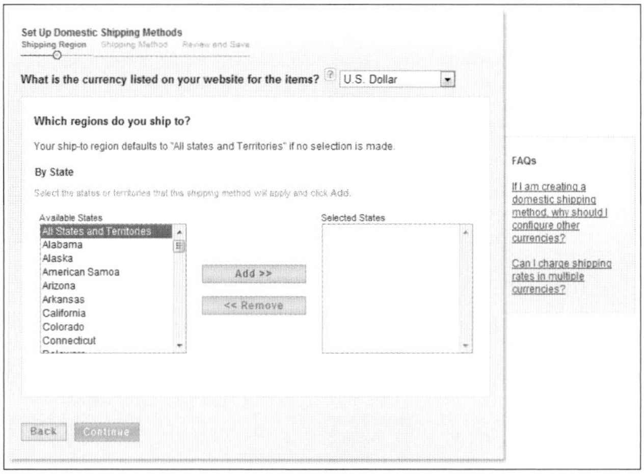

Figure 4.8
Specifying where you ship.

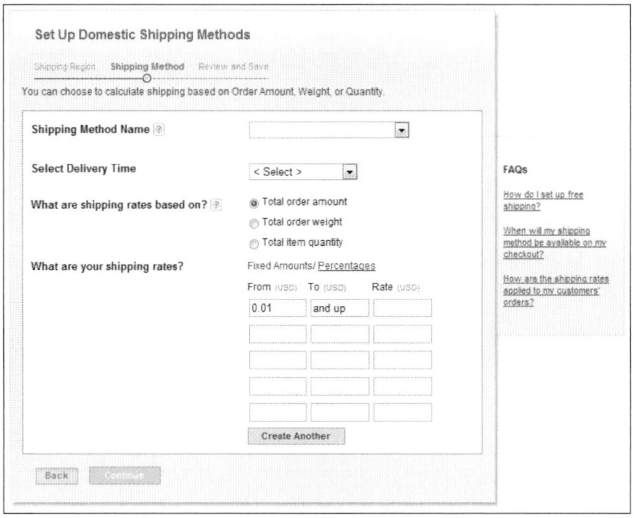

Figure 4.9
Specifying how you ship—and how much you charge for shipping.

PayPal now displays the Review and Save page, like the one shown in **Figure 4.10**. If what you see is correct, click the Save Shipping Methods button.

Customizing the Payment Confirmation Page

By default, PayPal displays somewhat generic pages (with your business name at the top) to accept and confirm a customer's payment, like the one in **Figure 4.11**. That's fine for many businesses, but you may want to provide a more branded experience to your customers.

TIP: You can also set a specific shipping fee for individual SKUs on your site. In this instance, the shipping fee is hard-coded into the Add to Cart button for that product. Simply enter the shipping fee into the Shipping box when you create the button.

Figure 4.10
Reviewing your shipping settings.

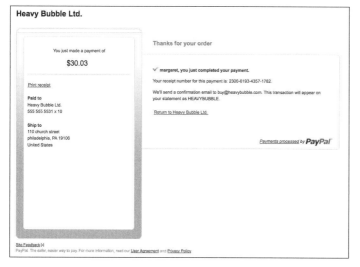

Figure 4.11
A standard payment confirmation page.

To that end, PayPal lets you customize the various checkout pages with your own logo, header image, and custom colors. Go to your profile, select My Selling Tools on the left, and under the Selling Online heading, click to update your Custom Payment Pages. When the Customize Your Payment Page appears, make sure you have the Page Styles tab selected, and then click the Add button.

When the Edit Custom Page Style page appears, all you have to do is fill in the blanks:

1. Enter a new name in the Page Style Name box.

2. Enter the URL for your logo image file in the Logo Image URL box. Your logo image file should be no larger than 190 pixels wide by 60 pixels high, and must be hosted on the Web, preferably on a secure server. This logo will appear at the top of the order summary.

3. Enter the HTML hex code for the desired page color in the Cart Area Gradient Color box.

4. Enter the URL for your desired header image in the Header Image URL box. Your header image file should be no larger than 750 pixels wide by 90 pixels high, and must be hosted on the Web, preferably on a secure server. This image will appear on the top left of the payment page.

5. Enter the HTML hex code for the desired header background color in the Header Background Color box.

6. Enter the HTML hex code for the desired header border color in the Header Border Color box.

7. Enter the HTML hex code for the desired background color for the payment page in the Background Color box.

8. Click the Preview button to see what your page will look like, and then click Save to save and apply the new template.

The result will look something like the page shown in **Figure 4.12**. Note the custom header image, and gradient color.

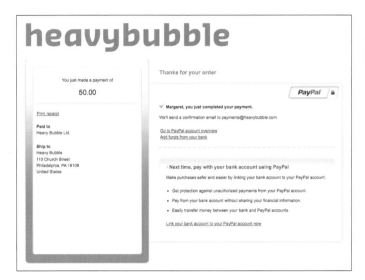

Figure 4.12
*A customized
payment page.*

Receiving Notification of Payment Activity

How do you know when a customer makes a purchase from your site?

If you're using the PayPal Shopping Cart, PayPal notifies you by email of all PayPal-related transactions—purchases and otherwise. If you're integrating PayPal into an existing shopping cart, PayPal will notify the shopping cart system directly—and can send you an email notification, as well. In particular, you're notified of

- Instant payments, including direct credit card payments.

- E-check payments and associated status.

- Recurring payment and subscription actions.

- Chargebacks, disputes, reversals, and refunds.

If you have a more sophisticated back-end system, you can take advantage of PayPal's Instant Payment Notification (IPN). This messaging service automatically notifies your system of all PayPal-related transactions, with no human intervention required.

NOTE: IPN messages duplicate messages also sent via email.

IPN messages are detected and processed via a listener script or program that is integrated into your back-end system. (You'll need to write your own listener scripts.) When the listener receives an IPN message, it then passes that message to the appropriate process to respond to the message. For example, an IPN message about a customer purchase can trigger order fulfillment processes, update your customer list, and update your accounting records. You can configure the IPN messages you receive by clicking the Instant Payment Notification Preferences link on your profile.

Configuring Other Options

There are several other options you can configure from the My Selling Tools area of your PayPal profile. These include

- **Selling Online**. This section includes a variety of links to help you manage your online selling activities. From here you can manage your PayPal payment buttons; change the company name that appears on your customers' credit card statements; set up sales tax options; configure PayPal payment pages to look more like your own website; determine which web pages customers are directed to after they pay with PayPal; manage API credentials for integrating PayPal with your own online store or shopping cart; and create and manage your invoice templates.

- **Getting Paid and Managing My Risk**. This section includes a variety of links to help you manage customer payments. From here you can manage subscriptions and other automatic payments; integrate PayPal's instant payment notifications with your website; manage PayPal's risk and fraud controls to automatically accept or decline certain types of payments; block payments based on specified criteria; and create a personalized message to use when faced with customer disputes.

- **Shipping My Items**. This section helps you configure PayPal's shipping functionality. From here you can edit your shipping preferences, including carriers and labels, as well as set up shipping methods and pricing for each of your customers.

You'll also find links to additional selling tools, including encrypted payment settings, PayPal button language encoding, PayPal shops, and your seller reputation number.

NOTE: Your Seller Reputation Number reflects the number of unique verified PayPal members who have paid you.

The three other entries on the left panel of your profile pertain to any PayPal member—they are not specific to a business that is selling through PayPal. These are:

- **My Business Info**. Where you edit your contact information such as email address, phone number.

- **My Money**. Where you set your payment and banking information, including credit card and bank account numbers.

- **My Settings**. Where you will find your basic account settings such as notifications, customer ID, and so forth.

Dealing with Foreign Currency Transactions

If you do business outside the United States, there are two ways to handle payments in foreign currencies. You can either keep payments in foreign currency and then convert those payments at some point to withdraw them, or you can have payments automatically converted into your primary currency at the time of the transaction.

As such, you can use PayPal to help you deal with foreign currency transactions. There are two primary settings you'll want to configure.

Managing Currency Balances

For day-to-day management of foreign currency transactions, go to your profile, click My Money on the left, and look for the line displaying your PayPal balance. At the end of that line, instead of the usual Update link,

Figure 4.13

Managing foreign currencies.

there is an invitation to see More, with a downward arrow. When you hover over this, click the Currencies link which appears—displaying the Manage Currencies page, shown in **Figure 4.13**. From here you can add new currencies, select your primary currency, and convert funds from one currency to another.

Accepting or Denying Cross-Currency Payments

You can also configure your PayPal account to accept or deny payments from selected currencies. When a customer pays in a currency you accept, funds appear in your PayPal account in the balance for that currency. When a customer tries to pay in a currency that you do not accept, you can opt to accept or deny that payment.

To configure these settings, go to your profile and click the My Selling Tools option on the left. Under the Getting Paid and Managing My Risk heading, update how you want to block payments. The Payment Receiving Preferences page appears. Here, you will see an option to "Block payments sent to me in a currency I do not hold." You can check Yes to block these payments; check No to accept them and convert them to U.S. dollars; or check Ask Me if you want to determine your course of action on a case-by-case basis.

Recurring Payments

PayPal also enables you to offer subscriptions and other services that depend on recurring payments, such as service and support plans, automatic product upgrades, monthly club memberships, payment plans, and the like.

For example, an electronics retailer might want to offer an enhanced support plan for customers who purchase a particular product. The merchant charges $9.95 per month for this plan. The retailer can set up PayPal's recurring payments to automatically charge customers this amount each month.

As another example, a camera retailer might offer an email newsletter for aficionados of a particular type of photography, such as nature or sports photography, and charge $4.99 for each monthly issue. This merchant can set up PayPal's recurring payments to automatically charge subscribers this amount each month.

PayPal's recurring payments are available with all of PayPal's payment processing solutions: Website Payments Standard, Website Payments Pro, and Express Checkout. With the basic Website Payments Standard there is no charge for the recurring payments service, aside from normal PayPal transaction fees.

Adding a Subscribe Button to Your Site

With Website Payments Standard, you integrate recurring payments by creating a Subscribe button that you then add to your website, like the one in **Figure 4.14**. Follow these instructions:

Figure 4.14
A PayPal Subscribe button.

1. Log in to your PayPal account and select the Merchant Services tab.

2. Go to the Create Buttons section of the page and click the Subscribe link.

Figure 4.15

Creating a Subscribe button.

3. When the Create PayPal Payment button page appears, as shown in **Figure 4.15**, make sure Subscriptions is selected in the button type list.

4. Enter the item name and optional subscription ID in the appropriate boxes.

5. To customize the appearance of the button, click the "Customize text or appearance" link and make the appropriate selections.

6. If you want PayPal to create user names and passwords for your subscribers, check that option.

7. Enter the amount to be billed each cycle.

8. In the Billing Cycle section, select the billing cycle in terms of X number of periods.

9. Select after how many cycles the billing should stop.

10. If you want to offer a trial period, check that option and then enter the required information for the free or discounted trial.

11. Select which Merchant account ID this button should apply to.

12. Click the Create Button button.

13. This displays the HTML code for this button. Copy and paste the code into the web page(s) on your site where you want the button to appear.

Using the Recurring Payments API

With Website Payments Pro and Express Checkout, the process is a bit more involved. You have to create a recurring payments profile for the service or subscription offered, and implement the various Recurring Payment APIs in your checkout process. PayPal then automatically handles all payment activity for customers who sign up for what you offer.

See the PayPal Developer Network website (www.x.com) for detailed instructions.

Creating and Sending Customer Invoices

For many businesses, such as contractors and medical offices, you have to ask to get paid. That is, instead of customers paying directly when they purchase something from your website, you send out invoices after the fact for products sold or services rendered.

PayPal facilitates sending out invoices via Online Invoicing. This is an option with all PayPal payment solutions, or a service that can be used separately. You pay nothing for the invoicing service, only the typical PayPal transaction fees when your customer pays.

Creating an Invoice

If you only do occasional invoicing, you can create and send single invoices with relative ease. Follow these steps:

1. Log in to your PayPal account and click the Request Money tab.

2. Select the Create Invoice subtab.

3. When the Create a New Invoice page appears, it uses the default template. To change this, use the pull down to select another template. (If you have not set up any templates yet, we'll get to that shortly.)

4. Confirm your contact information, and enter your recipient's email address—which can be selected from your Address Book.

5. Enter the overall attributes of the invoice (invoice number, date, and so forth as shown in **Figure 4.16**).

Figure 4.16

Enter overall invoice information.

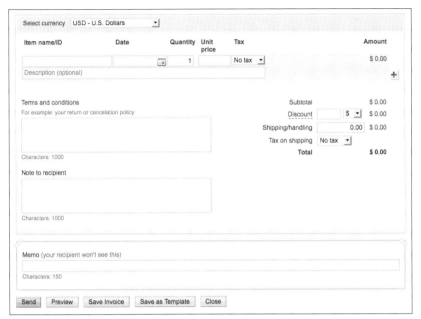

Figure 4.17
*Adding line items
and other details to
the invoice.*

6. Further down on the same page (shown in **Figure 4.17**), select the appropriate currency and start entering items for your invoice. Enter the item ID, date, quantity, unit price, and optional description for each item billed. You should also select if this is a taxable item. Use the plus sign to add additional items as needed.

7. Enter any applicable discount, shipping, and tax information. Add your terms, and any desired notes to recipient. The memo field is available for your internal notes which will not be seen by the customer.

8. At the bottom of Figure 4.17, you can see five options for next steps:

    Send, to send the invoice to your customer
    Preview, to see what the customer will be able to see
    Save Invoice, to keep for sending later (perhaps after additional editing)
    Save as Template, to conveniently send similar invoices later
    Close, to exit from the screen without saving

The customer now receives your invoice via email. The invoice includes a PayPal payment button; to pay the invoice, the customer simply clicks this button and is taken to the PayPal site where payment can be made via credit card, bank account, or the customer's PayPal account.

Creating an Invoice Template

If you do a lot of online invoicing, it helps to create templates for your most common invoice types. This speeds up the invoice creation process over time.

As noted previously, you can create a template based on any invoice you send. You can also create templates from scratch. The process is similar to creating a new invoice. Follow these steps:

1. Log in to your PayPal account and click the Request Money tab.

2. Select the Invoice Settings subtab.

3. When the Invoice Templates page appears, click the Add button.

4. When the Create Invoice Template page appears, select an existing template on which to base this new template, and then click the Continue button.

5. When the next page appears, enter all necessary information about the invoice recipient and items to be billed, and then click the Continue button.

6. When the Preview Invoice Template page appears, click the Save Template button.

This invoice template now appears in your list of saved templates.

Managing Your Invoices

You can track your invoice activity from the invoice History page. Access this page by going to the Request Money tab and then clicking the Manage Invoices subtab.

As you can see in **Figure 4.18**, the History page lists all recent invoices you've sent. Each listing includes the date sent, type of invoice, recipient's email address, payment status, and PayPal fees due on this transaction. You can filter the invoices by payments sent, payments received, and the like; just click the More Filters list and make a selection.

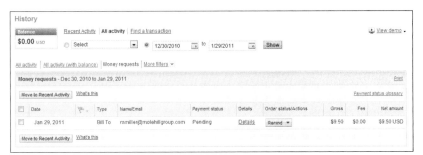

Figure 4.18
Managing invoice activity.

To perform an action on a given invoice, select an option in the Order Status/Actions column for that item. You can, for example, send a reminder notice or cancel a transaction. To view the complete invoice, click the Details link.

The Bottom Line

For most merchants, customers pay via an online shopping cart and checkout system. You can build your own shopping cart as part of your e-commerce website, contract with a third-party to provide shopping cart services, or use the PayPal Shopping Cart included free with PayPal's Website Payments Standard. When you use the PayPal Shopping Cart, you can specify taxes and shipping fees, customize the payment pages your customers see, and configure how you deal with transactions in foreign currencies.

If you offer subscriptions or other services that require recurring payments, PayPal lets you add a Subscription button to your site, along with corresponding information on the recurring payments. And if your business is one where the customer is billed for goods or services, you can use PayPal's Online Invoicing to email invoices to your customers; customers can pay the invoice by clicking the PayPal payment button included within it.

5

Pricing

If you have your own shopping cart or content management system on your website, you control all aspects of product pricing; the price you set is transmitted to the shopping cart when the customer makes a purchase. PayPal only sees the total value in the shopping cart when it comes time to process the customer's payment.

If you use the PayPal Shopping Cart, however, PayPal becomes an integral part of your pricing process. That's because you set the price for each item when you create the item's payment button; PayPal picks up the price you set and uses it throughout the balance of the checkout process.

How Product Pricing Works

When you use PayPal's Website Payments Standard, with the accompanying PayPal Shopping Cart, pricing information about each item you sell is hard-coded into the payment button you create for that item. This is true for both single-item sites (the Buy Now button) or sites offering multiple SKUs (the Add to Cart button).

When a customer clicks the Buy Now or Add to Cart button, the price of that item (along with other product information, such as color or size) is transmitted to PayPal and stored in the PayPal Shopping Cart. The price you set is included in the calculations when the customer checks out and pays.

CAUTION: PayPal only knows what it reads in the button code. If no information is present, PayPal can't charge your customer for the item.

This means, of course, that if you enter the wrong price for an item when you're creating its payment button, that incorrect price will be used when PayPal is calculating the amount due from the customer. It doesn't matter if the product web page says the item price is $9.99, if you mistakenly coded the payment button at a price of $999.99, the customer will be billed the incorrect price. (PayPal is only as accurate as you are.)

It's imperative, then, that you have accurate pricing available when you generate the code for your PayPal payment buttons. You have to get the pricing right when you create a button—or regenerate the button code with updated pricing information.

Note that you can assign multiple prices to a single button. This is useful if you sell an item in different sizes or colors, or with different options; you can charge different prices for different variations. The customer will see a pull-down list of the available options, with the price for each option listed. When the customer makes a selection from the list, the price for the selected variation is transmitted to the PayPal Shopping Cart.

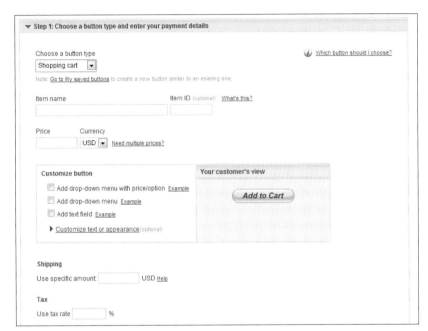

Figure 5.1
Creating an Add to Cart button, complete with item price.

Setting Product Pricing

You set your product pricing when you create the payment button for a given item, as shown in **Figure 5.1**.

You learned how to create a payment button in Chapter 3, "Integrating PayPal with Your Site," so those details won't be repeated here. Basically, you fill in the Price box and choose the desired currency.

It gets a bit more complicated when you have different prices for an item depending on options selected. In this instance, follow these steps:

1. While creating the button, leave the Price box blank and go directly to the Customize Button section.

2. Check the Add Drop-Down Menu with Price/Option box. This expands the Customize Button section as shown in **Figure 5.2** (on the next page).

3. Enter a name for this drop-down menu. For example, if you offer an item in different sizes, name the menu "Sizes." If you offer an item in different colors, name the menu "Colors."

Figure 5.2

Specifying different prices for different product options.

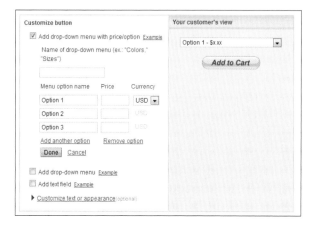

4. Go to the first Menu Option Name box and enter the text for the first option.

5. Enter the price for the first option in the first Price box.

6. Repeat Steps 4 and 5 for additional options and prices; click the Add Another Option link if you have more than three variations.

7. Continue with the rest of the button-creation process as normal.

Figure 5.3

A pull-down menu for an item with different sizes available (at different prices).

What you end up with is a button with a drop-down menu that looks something like the one in **Figure 5.3**. The customer makes a selection from the drop-down menu, and the code for that selection (which includes the price) is then transmitted to the PayPal Shopping Cart.

Setting Subscription Pricing

What do you do if you offer a subscription-based product, or one that requires recurring billing? Maybe you publish a print or online newsletter that sells for *x* dollars a month. Or maybe you sell a maintenance plan for a certain product that costs *x* dollars a year. In either case, you need to sign up your customers to pay you a set amount each time period, automatically.

Not surprisingly, PayPal's price-setting process is similar for subscription-based sales. You specify the price of the subscription and that price is hard-coded into the Subscribe button.

Figure 5.4
Creating a Subscribe button.

The big difference with subscriptions is that you need to specify the billing period (every *x* number of days, weeks, months, or years). You can also offer a trial period, so that customers can get a free or reduced-price view before they commit to a full subscription.

To set subscription pricing, follow these steps:

1. Begin the button creation process as normal.

2. Pull down the Choose a Button Type list and select Subscriptions. The page changes to that shown in **Figure 5.4**.

3. Enter the subscription name and identifying number into the Item Name and Subscription ID boxes.

4. Select the desired currency from the Currency list.

5. Enter the regular billing amount into the Billing Amount Each Cycle box.

6. Go to the Billing Cycle section and select your billing cycle—how often you bill, in *x* number of days, weeks, months, or years.

7. Set the length of the subscription in the After How Many Cycles Should Billing Stop list.

8. If you offer a trial period at a free or reduced price, check "I want to offer a trial period." Enter the charge for the trial period; if it's a free trial, enter "0." Then, under Define the trial period, enter the length of the trial period.

9. If you want to offer a second trial period, check that option, and then fill in the necessary information.

10. Continue with the rest of the button creation process as normal.

Changing Prices

Since your pricing is hard-coded into the PayPal payment buttons, what do you do when you need to change prices? You have a few options.

Creating a Replacement Button

First, you can simply create a new button for the item at the new price. You then replace the existing button code on your web page with this new button code.

This process is made easier if you save the buttons you create, which is an option when you create each one. Here's how to create a new button from a saved button:

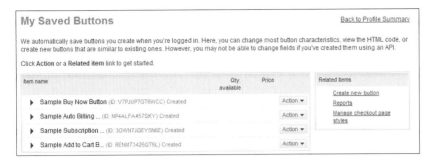

Figure 5.5 *Viewing saved buttons. The link to this screen is in your profile.*

1. Log in to your PayPal account, click the My Account tab, then select the Profile subtab.

2. When your profile appears, click My Selling Tools on the left to display those settings. Under the Selling Online heading, click to update your PayPal buttons.

3. When the My Saved Buttons page appears, as shown in **Figure 5.5**, click the Action button for the button you wish to change and select Edit Button.

4. When the Edit Your PayPal Button page appears, change the price as necessary.

5. Click the Save Changes button when done.

Editing Button Code

If you're fluent in HTML code, you can edit the button code on your website to change the associated price. The button code itself is a block of code that starts with the following line, or something similar:

```
<form target="paypal" action="https://www.paypal.com/cgi-bin/
→webscr" method="post">
```

Within the block of code, look for the line or lines that include the value variable. This variable should be followed by a price, like this:

```
value="9.99"
```

In an Add to Cart button, this variable is included in an input line, similar to this one:

```
<input type="hidden" name="amount" value="9.99">
```

NOTE: If an SKU has multiple prices for different options, you'll see multiple value variables, one for each option. You'll need to change all relevant value variables.

Once you've located the value variable and its associated value, simply change the value to the item's new price. Once you save the web page and take it live, the new price will be transmitted the next time a customer clicks on the payment button.

Edit this HTML with care—you can cause serious problems by simply forgetting to close quotation marks! Also, there is a unique identifier for every button that you must leave as provided by PayPal.

What's the Right Price?

It's a good idea to do your market research before you set your product pricing—and to monitor the competition's prices on an ongoing basis. You can do this manually, by going to your competitors' websites and seeing what they're charging for the same or similar items. You can also take advantage of the pricing research services offered by various market research firms.

Some pricing research is quantitative; actual pricing data is pulled from the Web. Other pricing research is qualitative, in that customers are asked, via survey or focus group, how much they're willing to pay for a given product or service. Naturally, the qualitative research is more costly, and less reliable. (People don't always act the way they say they will when questioned.)

Whatever type of research you do, know that elements other than price play a role in how much a customer is willing to pay for an item. You also have to consider the other services you offer, the selection you carry, how fast you ship, the quality of your customer service, and your reputation. Sometimes you can charge a little more if you offer more in terms of selection or service; some customers are willing to pay a higher price for a quality experience.

And remember, pricing is not static. Competitors raise and lower prices all the time; new competitors can also muddy the waters. Product pricing is not a "set it and forget it" operation; be prepared to update your PayPal payment buttons as necessary to accommodate pricing changes.

Finally, know that you can't charge your customers extra when they pay via PayPal. Adding this sort of surcharge violates your PayPal agreement, and isn't good business, in any case. You don't want to penalize customers for choosing one payment method over another.

The Bottom Line

When you use PayPal's Website Payments Standard, pricing information is hard-coded into a product's payment button. The product price is then transmitted to PayPal when a customer clicks the payment button. You can configure your payment buttons for products with multiple options, such as size and color, and different prices for each option. In addition, if you offer subscription services, you can set different subscription periods as well as trial subscriptions. When a product's price changes, simply generate a new button code for that item—or edit the existing button code on your website.

6

Processing Purchases

Processing customer purchases is the end result of the checkout procedure, and the key to the efficient operation of any e-commerce website. Payment information must be collected, the payment must be processed, and information must be provided to the retailer for shipping and inventory management.

How you process the purchase depends on your checkout and payment processing solutions. For example, with Website Payments Pro and PayPal's Payflow Payment Gateway solutions, processing customer orders is part of your existing checkout system; PayPal really doesn't get involved. With PayPal's Website Payments Standard and Express Checkout, on the other hand, the processing happens primarily on PayPal's website.

Processing Purchases with Website Payments Standard

Let's first look at how the processing of orders works with Website Payments Standard, PayPal's HTML-based payment solution designed for small and medium-sized merchants. The customer order is transmitted to PayPal; PayPal then processes payment and transmits key order information back to the merchant. As a merchant, you need to be prepared to receive this information—and to act on it.

With Website Payments Standard, the order commences not when items have been placed into the customer's shopping cart (by clicking Add to Cart buttons), but rather when the customer goes to the PayPal Shopping Cart to check out.

Of course, you need to make it easy for customers to access the shopping cart. This means inserting View Cart buttons on all of your product pages, as well as other relevant pages on your site. The View Cart button should be placed in a prominent position on the page; you want your customers to see it so they can check out and pay.

NOTE: You need only generate a single View Cart button code. This code is then inserted multiple times on your site, wherever you want the View Cart button to appear.

Placing the Order

When a customer clicks the View Cart button, she is redirected to the PayPal site, and PayPal displays a shopping cart page, like the one in **Figure 6.1**. After reviewing the contents of the cart, the customer can click the Continue Shopping button to be redirected back to your site for additional shopping (and, hopefully, more ordering) or click the Proceed to Checkout button to pay for the items currently in the cart.

When the Proceed to Checkout button is clicked, PayPal displays a billing information/login page, like the one shown in **Figure 6.2**. From here the customer can log in to her PayPal account to pay in that fashion, or directly enter credit card and shipping information here.

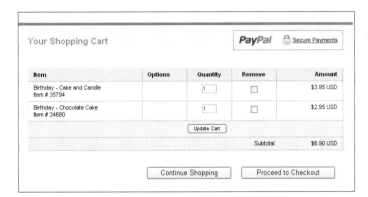

Figure 6.1

A typical shopping cart page.

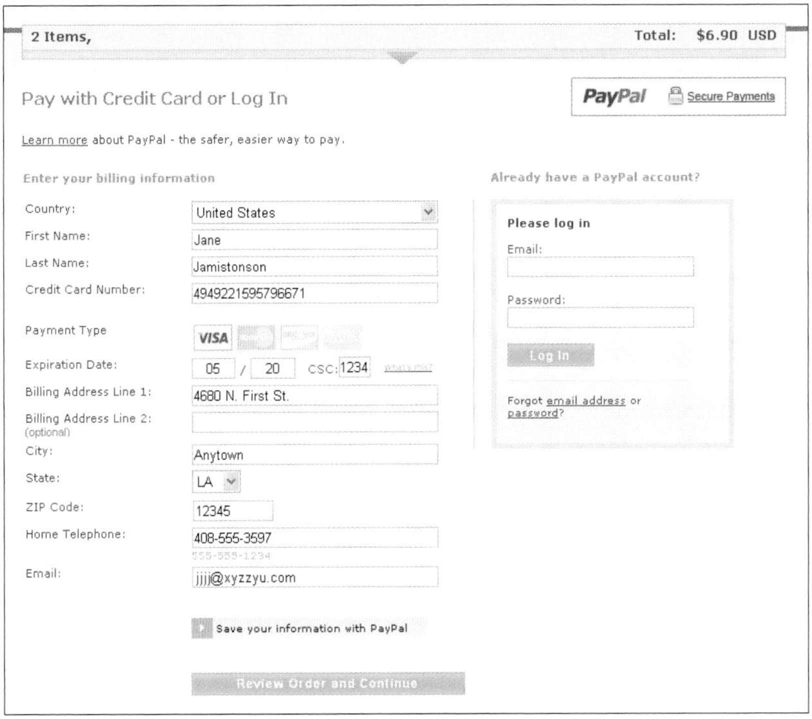

Figure 6.2

A typical billing information page.

If the customer logs in to her PayPal account, payment and shipping information are pulled from her account and applied to this order; it's a relatively quick process for the customer. If the customer chooses to pay by credit card without accessing a PayPal account, there's more work required in the way of entering the necessary information into the form.

Reviewing the Order

However the customer chooses to pay, PayPal displays a transaction confirmation page, like the one in **Figure 6.3**. This provides the customer with a final opportunity to make changes to her order or shipping information, and to change the method of payment (when paying via PayPal).

Once all the details are finalized, the customer clicks the Pay Now button on this page. This transmits the relevant customer data to PayPal.

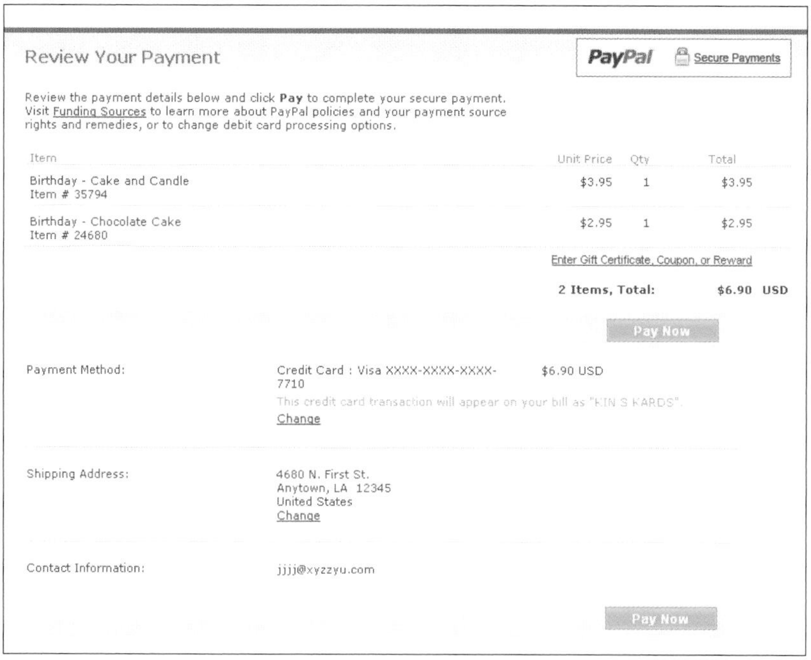

Figure 6.3

A typical transaction confirmation page.

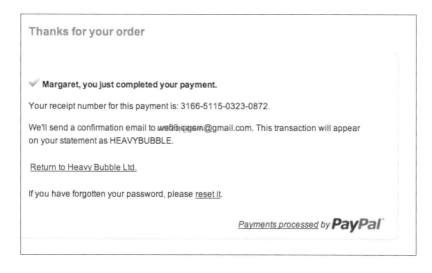

Figure 6.4
A typical payment confirmation page.

Processing the Payment

At this point, PayPal processes the payment, based on the payment method selected by the customer—credit card, debit card, or electronic bank withdrawal. Payment processing involves contacting the customer's credit card company or bank to ensure that the customer's credit line is high enough (or enough funds are currently available) to pay for the transaction.

What happens next depends on whether or not the transaction is approved:

- If the transaction is approved, PayPal authorizes the payment, and funds are transferred from the customer's credit card or bank account to PayPal.

- If the transaction is not approved, PayPal displays a message notifying the customer of this fact and asking for a different form of payment.

Assuming credit authorization, PayPal displays the payment confirmation page, shown in **Figure 6.4**. At this point the customer can choose to print a copy of the receipt, or return to the merchant's website.

That's the end of the process as far as the customer is concerned, but there's more happening on the back-end.

NOTE: PayPal also emails a payment authorization notice to the customer. This provides additional confirmation of the transaction.

Notifying the Merchant

After the customer transaction is concluded, PayPal does two more things.

First, PayPal deposits the appropriate funds from the transaction (minus applicable transaction fees) into your PayPal account, assuming it is in good standing.

Second, PayPal notifies you of the transaction. This notification can take place via email or automated electronic message. The former method is done by default; the latter must be implemented via special code on your website. The transaction also shows up in your PayPal account overview.

RECEIVING NOTIFICATION VIA EMAIL

By default, PayPal notifies you via email of all customer transactions. Email notifications are sent to your primary email address, unless you've configured your account otherwise. PayPal sends email notifications when the following activities occur:

- Payments are made.

- Payments are pending.

- Payments are cancelled.

Naturally, you need to be on the lookout for these email notifications from PayPal. You don't need to monitor your email inbox every minute of every day, but you do need to respond to these notifications promptly to ensure the best possible customer service.

CAUTION: The worst situation is missing an order because the email from PayPal ended up in your email application's spam folder. Make sure you configure your email program to accept all messages from the paypal.com domain.

RECEIVING NOTIFICATION VIA PDT

In addition to the default email notification, you can opt to receive information about transactions via Payment Data Transfer (PDT). PDT doesn't necessarily trigger any order processing activity on your part, but instead returns information about the transaction to your website. This, in turn, enables you to display information about the transaction to the customer.

For example, you can use the data sent via PDT to display a "thank you" page when the customer is redirected back to your site after concluding payment on the PayPal site. It's a nice way to personalize the transaction, and create a closer bond between you and your customers.

NOTE: Instructions for implementing PDT on your website are available from www.x.com, PayPal's Developer Network site.

When you activate PDT, PayPal creates a transaction token when the customer transaction is completed, at the same time that it displays the order confirmation page for the customer. This token is sent to the URL on your website that you specify in your account settings.

PDT is implemented via HTTP POST commands. (Your website developer will know how this works.) The transaction token sent via PDT contains key data about the customer and the item(s) purchased; this data is then used to populate a web page template.

RECEIVING NOTIFICATION VIA IPN

You can also opt to receive notification about shopping cart transactions and customer payment activity via a form of automated electronic messaging dubbed Instant Payment Notification (IPN). IPN messages are sent directly from PayPal to your web server, and can be handled on an automated basis.

IPN messages are sent by PayPal under the following conditions:

- Payments are first made, either completed or pending.

- Payments clear, fail, or are denied.

IPN is a great way to automate order processing, particularly fulfillment and customer tracking. If properly implemented, IPN reduces the reliance on human beings to notice and respond to messages regarding transactions.

Of course, to use IPN for order processing you have to activate it in your PayPal account. You also need to install a listener script on your website. The listener "listens" for IPN messages—and, when messages are received, passes them on to the appropriate processing functions on your site.

NOTE: PayPal provides sample code you can modify to implement a listener on your site. Visit www.x.com for more information.

Figure 6.5

How IPN is integrated into order processing.

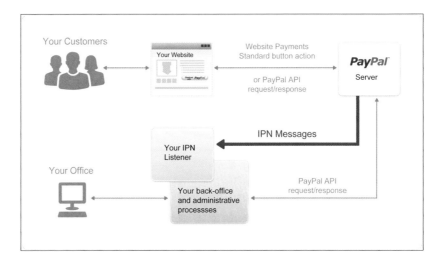

Figure 6.5 details how IPN works in regards to order processing. IPN can be used to trigger order fulfillment or enable media downloads when a transaction is concluded, or to update your customer list or accounting records.

NOTE: You can also track your customer order activity online at PayPal. To learn more, see Chapter 12, "Managing Business Info and Data."

Know that IPN is an asynchronous message service, which means that messages are not synchronized with actions on your website; PayPal has no way of knowing if a message was received or acted upon. Due to the possibility of lost or delayed messages, PayPal resends IPN messages at various intervals (up to four days after the transaction) until you acknowledge receipt. Because of this, you'll need to incorporate some sort of answering mechanism into the IPN-related code you add to your website.

Completing the Transaction

Once you receive notification of the transaction, the item(s) purchased can be shipped to the customer. Naturally, you should ship the order as soon as possible; it's simply good customer service.

NOTE: PayPal has various products that can assist with the shipping process. Learn more in Chapter 7, "Shipping Orders."

An Example Process

To get a better feel for what's involved, let's look at a fictitious example of the Website Payments Standard purchase process.

Customer Sherry Jones visits the Super Big Shoestore website. Super Big Shoestore uses PayPal Website Payments Standard, and has inserted Add to Cart buttons on all of its product pages.

Sherry decides to purchase a pair of red pumps priced at $99. She clicks the Add to Cart button for that item. The information embedded in that item's button is transmitted to PayPal, which places the product and pricing data in a temporary shopping cart.

Sherry continues shopping and finds a second pair of shoes, a pair of tan sandals, priced at $79. She clicks the Add to Cart button for this item, and the data for this item is also transmitted to PayPal and placed in Sherry's shopping cart.

PayPal INSIDER

 ### Automating Processing of Orders

Once your volume reaches a certain level, manual processing of transactions becomes unwieldy, with the result that your order fulfillment times become longer than customers might accept. The solution, of course, is to automate your order processing activities—which is where IPN comes in.

When used properly, IPN can eliminate a lot of manual activity from your order processing. With IPN, you don't need to manually check your inbox for orders; IPN orders are sent directly to your website, where appropriate actions can be initiated.

The key to implementing IPN to process orders is adding code to your site that automatically acts on specific IPN messages. For example, when you receive an IPN message notifying you of a completed transaction, you want your site to receive the message, initiate the shipping process for the items purchased, remove the items from your inventory, and add the customer information to your database or mailing list. When done properly, IPN can truly automate your processing procedures.

Merchants who implement IPN can process more orders faster than merchants who do it the old-fashioned way. You'll have to do some programming on your end, and you'll need to construct the appropriate back-end systems, but it pays dividends in the form of more efficient operations. And if you can process and ship orders faster than your nonautomated competitors, that's a real marketplace advantage.

Sherry is now ready to check out and pay for her purchases. She clicks the View Cart button, prominently displayed on all of the site's product pages. Doing so redirects Sherry to PayPal's website, which displays her dynamically generated shopping cart page. Sherry looks over the two items in her cart and clicks the Proceed to Checkout button.

PayPal now displays a billing information page. Sherry is not yet a PayPal user, so she opts to pay by MasterCard. She enters her credit card information along with her street address and other shipping details, and then clicks the Review Order and Continue button. Sherry checks the information on the Review Your Payment page, and then clicks the Pay Now button.

This transmits the information Sherry entered to PayPal, which processes the credit card information and receives authorization for the transaction. PayPal now displays a payment confirmation page and sends an email to Sherry confirming the order. Sherry clicks the Continue button on the confirmation page and is returned to the Super Big Shoestore website.

As soon as PayPal receives authorization for Sherry's credit card payment, it transfers funds into Super Big Shoestore's account and sends an email to Super Big, notifying the company of the transaction. The email includes all relevant details, including the amount paid, the items ordered, and Sherry's shipping address.

A staffer at Super Big Shoestore checks his email inbox once an hour, and soon enough sees the email from PayPal concerning Sherry's transaction. He then initiates the packing and shipping of the items, and makes note of the transaction in the day's receipts. Later, another staffer withdraws the funds generated from Sherry's transaction, as part of a regular funds withdrawal.

And that completes the processing of Sherry's purchase—the order will be complete when she receives the shoes in the mail a few days later. She's happy with her experience, and pleased with the ease of the transaction.

Processing Purchases with Website Payments Pro

So far we've discussed how the processing of purchases works with Website Payments Standard, the preferred solution for many small and mid-sized businesses. If you're a larger business, however, or use a third-party shopping cart, Website Payments Pro may be more suitable for you.

Processing orders with Website Payments Pro is similar to Website Payments Standard, at least from the customer's perspective. But the back-end process is somewhat different—and depends on whether the customer is using PayPal's Direct Payment or Express Checkout.

Processing Direct Payments

Direct Payment is the part of Website Payments Pro that enables customers who do not have (or do not want to use) a PayPal account to pay via credit card without leaving your website. PayPal processes the credit card payment in the background while the customer remains in your standard checkout flow.

In this scenario, customers use your site's shopping cart to select individual items to purchase. When they check out, they're presented with a billing information page of your own design. Even though it's your billing information page, it must collect the following information to send to PayPal:

- Total amount of the transaction, including shipping/handling charges and sales tax

- Credit card type (MasterCard, Visa, American Express, or the like)

- Credit card number

- Credit card expiration date

- Credit card CSC (card security code)

- Cardholder first and last name

- Cardholder billing address (can be different from shipping address)

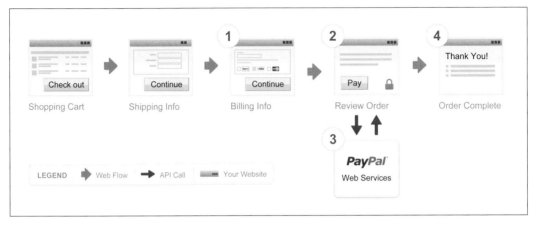

Figure 6.6 *Order processing with PayPal Direct Payment.*

When the customer clicks the Pay button on your site, this information is transmitted to PayPal automatically via the DoDirectPayment function in the API. (Your tech folks will know what this is, and can tie it into your systems during the integration phase.) PayPal then processes the credit card payment and, when authorization is received, passes the appropriate information (including the PayPal transaction ID) back to your site. Your site then displays a confirmation page to the customer and continues with the balance of the order process.

As you can see in **Figure 6.6**, the customer never leaves your website throughout this entire process. Although PayPal processes the payment, the customer is unaware of PayPal's involvement. In fact, the name "PayPal" doesn't even appear on the buyer's credit card statement. As far as the customer is concerned, she dealt with you throughout the entire process.

Processing Express Checkout Payments

Most merchants who use Website Payments Pro also employ Express Checkout. This checkout solution is targeted to existing PayPal customers who want to pay quickly and easily using the information stored in their PayPal accounts.

As with Direct Payment, customers use the ordering apparatus on your site to add items to your hosted shopping cart. When the customer begins the checkout process, she's presented with a Checkout with PayPal button.

Clicking this button redirects the customer to the PayPal site, where she's prompted to sign in with her PayPal ID and password.

PayPal then displays a transaction review page, which contains information about the customer's chosen payment method(s) stored on the PayPal site. The customer confirms the payment method (but doesn't have to reenter any credit card information), and is then returned to your site. Your site displays an order confirmation page; when the customer clicks the Pay Now button, transaction details (total order amount) are transmitted to PayPal.

PayPal links the transaction details with the customer's payment information and receives authorization for the transaction. This authorization is then transmitted to your site, where it's used to display a confirmation page to the customer. You can then proceed with the balance of the order process.

Figure 6.7 shows how this process works. The only time the customer leaves your site is to sign in to PayPal and confirm or choose a payment method. The rest of the process is hosted on your website; you remain in control of the customer experience.

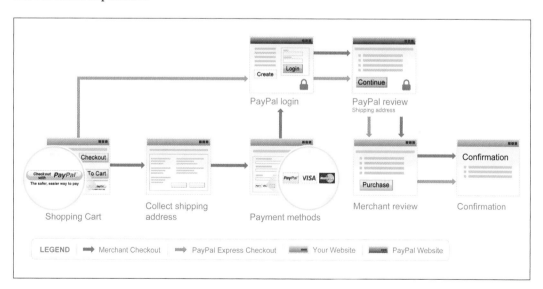

Figure 6.7 *Order processing with PayPal Express Checkout.*

The Bottom Line

Processing a purchase involves everything from the customer entering the checkout system to the completion of the transaction, including payment processing. With PayPal's Website Payments Standard, the payment procedure takes place on PayPal's site, based on information that is hard-coded into each item's Add to Cart button, options selected in the merchant's PayPal account, and information entered by the customer. With PayPal's Website Payments Pro, the entire process takes place on the merchant's website—except for payment processing, which is fed to and provided by PayPal.

At the conclusion of the purchase process, information is provided to the merchant that triggers the next step in the order process—packing and shipping—which we'll talk about in the next chapter.

7

Shipping Orders

From the customer's standpoint, the checkout process is just a small part of a transaction. Granted, it's the part where he pays for what he bought, but that's just a minor inconvenience. Much more important—and certainly more fun— is the part where the customer receives the item(s) he purchased.

Which brings us right to the process of shipping those orders you receive. PayPal is intimately involved with several parts of the shipping process, starting right up front—where you decide how much you're going to charge the customer for shipping.

Configuring Shipping Options for Website Payments Standard

As noted in Chapter 4, "Getting Paid," you set up a lot of information about your business when you first create your PayPal business account. Among the most important of these details are your shipping rates—how much you charge to ship items to your customers.

When you're using Website Payments Standard, PayPal lets you set universal shipping rates for all items purchased on your site. You can charge by the item, by the pound, by type of service used—you can even configure your account to offer free shipping on certain types of orders. It's all a matter of the settings you choose.

To configure your universal shipping settings: go to your profile, click My Selling Tools, and then, under the Shipping My Items heading, update your Shipping Calculations. From the Shipping Calculations page, shown in **Figure 7.1**, you can set up domestic and international shipping separately. We'll deal with domestic shipping first, and save non-U.S. shipping for the "Shipping Internationally" section later in this chapter. Click the Start button in the Set Up Domestic Shipping Methods section to begin setting your options.

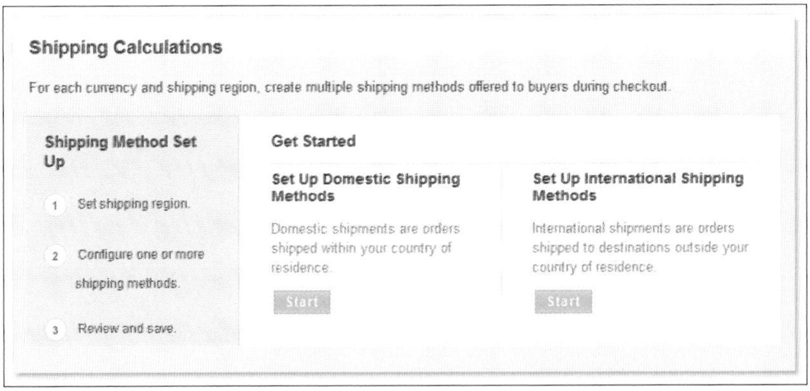

Figure 7.1

Getting ready to configure shipping options.

Shipping Calculations

For each currency and shipping region, create multiple shipping methods offered to buyers during checkout.

Shipping Method Set Up

1. Set shipping region.
2. Configure one or more shipping methods.
3. Review and save.

Get Started

Set Up Domestic Shipping Methods

Domestic shipments are orders shipped within your country of residence.

Start

Set Up International Shipping Methods

International shipments are orders shipped to destinations outside your country of residence.

Start

Selecting Where You Ship To

The first shipping option to configure is which locations you ship to. When you see the Shipping Region page, shown in **Figure 7.2**, select the states and territories you ship to. By default, PayPal assumes you ship to All States and Territories, but this is easy enough to change. If you only ship to selected states, select those states in the Available States list and click the Add button. This places them in the Selected States list—the list of states where you do offer shipping services. Click Continue when done.

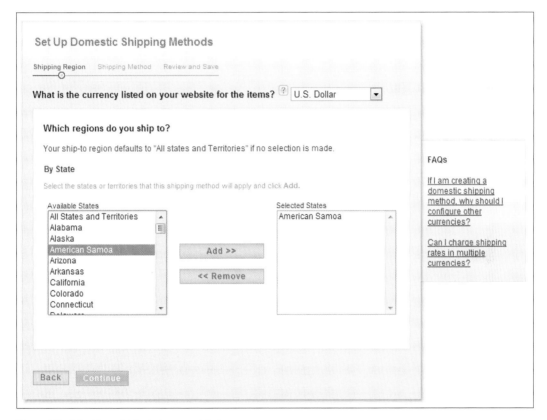

Figure 7.2 *Selecting which states you ship to.*

Selecting a Shipping Method

Next, you need to tell PayPal what shipping methods you offer. The Shipping Method page, shown in **Figure 7.3**, lets you specify the types of shipping you offer, and then set rates for each of them.

You can offer as many different shipping methods as you like, or as are feasible. For example, you might offer standard ground shipping and some form of expedited shipping, and let customers make their choice during the checkout process. Obviously, you can charge more for the costlier services.

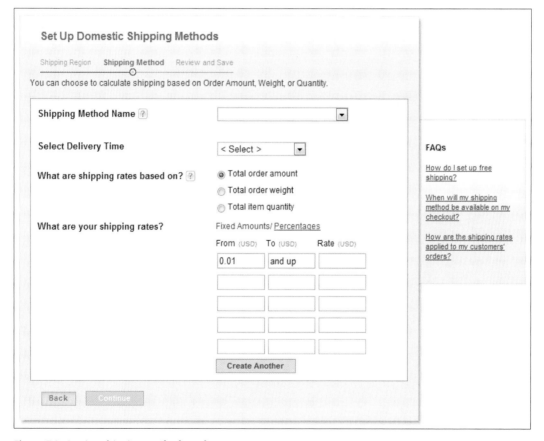

Figure 7.3 *Setting shipping methods and rates.*

What shipping methods can you offer? PayPal doesn't let you list specific services (UPS, FedEx, etc.), but rather more generic shipping types. Here's the list you can choose from:

- Air Service
- Economy
- Expedited Air Service
- Expedited Flat Rate Shipping
- Express
- Express Domestic
- Free Shipping
- Ground
- Global Priority
- International Economy
- International Expedited
- International Express
- International Express Air

- International Priority Air
- Next Day
- Next Day Air
- Next Day Air Economy
- One-Day Shipping
- Overnight
- Overnight Flat Rate Shipping
- Standard International
- Standard Shipping
- Store Pickup
- Two-Day Shipping
- Worldwide Shipping
- 2-Day Air

You should select the methods that best match the shipping services you typically use. For example, if you use U.S. Postal Service Parcel Post, you might specify Standard Shipping. If you use UPS Ground, you might specify Ground. Of course, if you offer free shipping, choose the Free Shipping option.

Whichever shipping method you choose, you also need to specify the typical delivery time for that option. Some combinations are obvious; if you select One-Day Shipping option, then you'd select One Business Day from the Select Delivery Time list. For other shipping methods, go with the average delivery time specified by the service you use.

NOTE: If you offer more than one shipping method, you'll need to click the Create Another button after you specify shipping rates for the first method. You can then enter different shipping rates for the next method.

Setting Shipping Rates

You now need to specify the exact shipping rates for each of your shipping methods. You base these rates on:

- **Total order amount.** For example, you could charge $5 shipping except for orders over $100 which would receive free shipping. You can set up as many price brackets as you like.

- **Total order weight.** For example, you could charge $5 for orders under 10 pounds and $10 for orders over 10 pounds—or simply charge $2 per pound.

- **Total order weight.** For example, you could charge $5 per item, or $5 for the first item and $2 for each subsequent item, and so forth.

You set your rates by filling in the boxes on the Shipping Method page. The box labels change according to how you determine your shipping

Choosing a Shipping Service

Whether you ship one package a week or hundreds of packages a day, you need to keep on top of your shipping costs. Don't assume that your current carrier offers the best solution; rates change constantly and another service might now offer better rates.

In most cases, you'll choose from one of the "big four" carriers—U.S. Postal Service, UPS, FedEx, and DHL—although, in some areas, regional carriers offer attractive rates. You'll need to examine services available, rates charged, and convenience. Some carriers might offer exactly what you need, others might be less compatible with your business. Examine all of the services offered by all of the carriers and make some hard comparisons.

Don't assume that you can't get a good deal if you're a smaller merchant. While larger

companies often do get rates up to 50 percent less than the standard walk-in rate, that doesn't mean those same or similar rates aren't available to you. Rather than just comparing rates on the carriers' websites, talk to a representative from each firm, lay out your shipping needs, and let him craft a cost-effective solution for you. And there's nothing that says you can't negotiate rates; it happens all the time, even with smaller businesses.

Once you've decided on a carrier, you still need to keep on top of the situation. With constantly changing shipping rates from the "big four," it's possible that today's good deal won't be quite as good tomorrow. Stay aware of current rates and revisit your shipping services on a regular basis. It's the smart thing to do.

rates, of course. If you select Total Order Amount, the boxes register U.S. dollars (USD). If you select Total Order Weight, the boxes register either pounds (lbs) or kilograms (kg). If you select Total Item Quantity, the boxes register the number of items.

Enter the lower range in the From box and the higher range in the To box, and then enter the shipping rate for this range into the Rate box. Use additional rows to enter rates for other ranges.

By the way, if you charge by total order amount, you can opt to calculate shipping on either a dollar rate or percentage basis. If you choose the

 ## Determining Your Shipping and Handling Charges

How do you decide how much to charge for shipping and handling? It's a trial-and-error process that benefits from a bit of research.

Start by examining the rate charts from the shipping services you use. Find out how much your shipping service charges to ship a one-pound package from your location to the farthest reaches of the U.S., and let that guide your shipping rates.

Know, however, that the cost to ship a particular package is based on a combination of weight, size, and distance; the heavier an item is and the further it has to go (and the faster you need it to get there), the more it costs. Once you start checking around, you'll find that shipping rates vary widely from one service to another.

Of course, you need to cover other expenses with these shipping fees. You'll want to consider the cost of the packaging you use—not just the box, but also the packing materials, sealing tape, labels, and so forth. You may also want to cover the labor costs involved with packing and shipping your items. Add these costs to the actual shipping costs incurred, and you have your total shipping and handling rate.

For some businesses shipping is a profit center. They deliberately charge their customers a little more than the shipping services cost. This is easy to do, as most customers don't know what the actual shipping charges are. Make sure not to gouge the customer, or charge rates too much higher than those of your competitors.

Other businesses view shipping as a competitive feature. That is, they pride themselves on their ultra-fast shipping, or on their free or reduced shipping rates. Let's face it; online customers are attracted to "free shipping" offers.

The bottom line is that shipping and handling charges are unique to each business. You can view it as a necessary evil, and pass exact costs on to your customers. You can view it as a profit center, and charge customers a little more than what it costs you. You can even view it as a competitive advantage, and offer free or reduced shipping to lure away business from the competition.

percentage option, you charge a set percentage of the total order amount for shipping. For example, if you charge 10 percent shipping, an order of $150 would be accompanied by a $15 shipping charge.

When you're done entering your shipping rates, click the Continue button. PayPal now displays the Review and Save page. Click the Save Shipping Methods button to finalize your settings.

Setting Shipping on an Item-by-Item Basis

While it's recommended that you establish sitewide shipping settings, you can set shipping fees for specific items. This lets you charge more for large or difficult-to-ship items, or offer free shipping on selected specials.

You set item-specific shipping rates while you're creating the item's Add to Cart button.

You can also set a specific shipping fee for individual SKUs on your site. In this instance, the shipping fee is hard-coded into the Add to Cart button for that product. Simply enter the shipping fee into the Shipping box when you create the button.

Figure 7.4 shows the PayPal button creation page for an Add to Cart button. Just enter the shipping rate for this item in the Shipping box. The rate entered here will override the universal shipping rates specified elsewhere, and be applied to the customer's order during the checkout process.

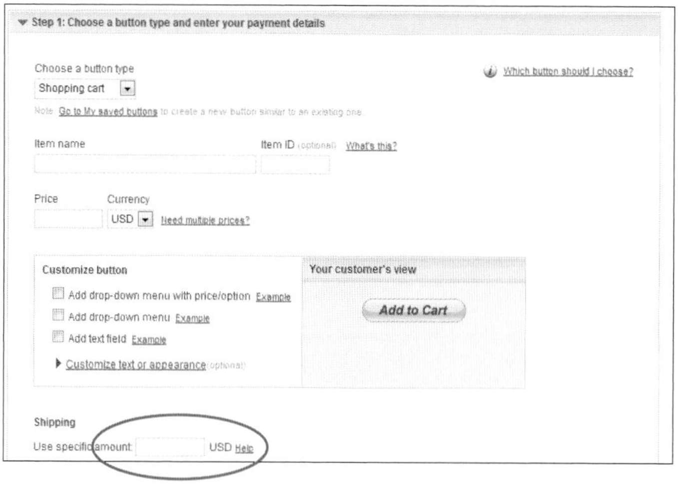

Figure 7.4

Setting the shipping rate for an individual SKU.

Shipping Your Orders

When it comes to shipping, PayPal's assistance doesn't end when the customer places an order. PayPal offers a variety of shipping tools to help you manage all your customer shipping needs, at no additional cost to you.

Printing a Packing Slip

The initial part of the shipping process involves preparing the item to ship. You'll want to include some sort of packing slip, of course; if you have your own company packing slips, that's great, otherwise you can print free packing slips from your PayPal account.

To print a PayPal packing slip, go to your account overview or History page, click on the individual transaction, then, when the Order Details page appears, scroll to the bottom of the page and click the Print Packing Slip link. This displays a packing slip page, like the one in **Figure 7.5**.

If you want to customize the packing slip, click the Edit button on the packing slip page. This displays the Edit Printable Packing Slip page, where you can opt to include your business's logo, address, phone number, and a personal message. To save your changes for all future packing slips, check the Save the Above Settings as My Packing Slip Preferences option; click the View Printable Packing Slip button to return to the main packing slip page. You can then click the Print button to print the packing slip.

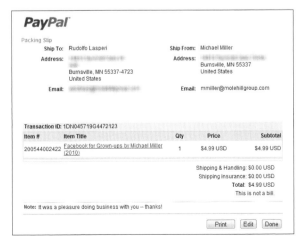

Figure 7.5

Printing a packing slip.

Packing the Order

Next, you need to pack the item (and its packing slip) in an appropriate shipping container. You have to choose the right type of container for each item you sell.

The first decision to make is whether to use a box or an envelope for shipping. If you have a very large item to ship, the choice is easy. But what if you have something smaller and flatter, such as a baseball card or a coin? Your choice should be determined by the fragility of your item. If the item can bend or break, choose a box; if not, an envelope is probably a safe choice.

Whichever you choose, pick a container that's large enough to hold your item without the need to force it in or bend it inappropriately. Also, make sure that the box has enough extra room to insert cushioning material. On the other hand, the container shouldn't be so big as to leave room for the item to bounce around. Also, you pay for size and weight; you don't want to pay to ship anything bigger or heavier than it needs to be.

TIP: After you pack your item, weigh and measure the package. You'll need this information when creating the postage-paid shipping label.

After you pack the item, you need to seal the box or envelope and affix the shipping label to the outside. Where does that shipping label come from? That's what we'll talk about next.

Shipping Individual Packages

PayPal lets you print shipping labels with prepaid postage for any item sold through the PayPal system. You can print labels one at a time, or batch multiple labels together with PayPal's MultiOrder Shipping. PayPal currently prints prepaid shipping labels for items shipped via the U.S. Postal Service, UPS, Canada Post, and the Royal Mail Group.

Let's start with one-at-a-time label printing. After an order has been processed (and payment received), follow these steps:

1. Log in to your PayPal account.

2. Click the My Account tab and select either the Overview or History subtab.

3. Click the Print Shipping Label button for this order.

Figure 7.6
*Entering shipment
information.*

4. When the Order Details page appears, scroll to the bottom of the page
    and click the Print Shipping Label link.

5. When the Create Your Shipping Label page appears, as shown in **Figure
    7.6**, confirm your desired shipping carrier. If you want to change car-
    riers for this shipment, click the Choose a Different Carrier link and
    make a new selection.

6. Select the specific shipping service from the Service Type list.

7. Select the approximate package size from the Package Size list.

8. Enter the weight of the package (in pounds and ounces) into the Weight boxes.

9. Review the shipping information in the Shipment Options sections, and make any necessary changes or selections.

10. Click the Continue button.

11. When the Confirm and Purchase Your Shipping Label page appears, confirm the information (and the shipping charges), and then click the Pay and Continue button.

12. PayPal now displays a pop-up window with a preview of the label to print, like the one in **Figure 7.7**. If everything looks fine, make sure you have label paper in your printer, and then click the Print Label button.

Figure 7.7

Printing a shipping label.

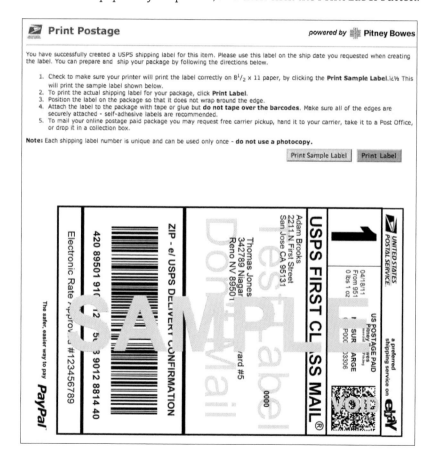

PayPal now prints the label and deducts the shipping cost from your account. Attach the label to your package and either drop it off at your nearest carrier office or arrange a pickup.

TIP: If you use a shipping service outside of PayPal, you can still enter tracking information into the PayPal system, so that the customer can track the shipment. Go to the Details section of the PayPal payment page and click the Add Tracking Information link.

Shipping Multiple Packages

If you ship many packages each day, you'll probably want to take advantage of PayPal's MultiOrder Shipping. This tool lets you print up to 50 prepaid shipping labels in a single batch. MultiOrder Shipping is a lot faster than printing one label at a time, a real time-saver for larger merchants—and, like other PayPal shipping tools, it's totally free.

CONFIGURING MULTIORDER SHIPPING

Before you use PayPal MultiOrder Shipping, you need to configure some settings. Follow these steps:

1. Log in to your PayPal account.

2. Click the Merchant Services tab.

3. On the next page, go to the Shipping & Tax section and click the MultiOrder Shipping link.

4. When the next page appears, click the Start Shipping button.

5. When MultiOrder Shipping opens in a new window, click Edit on the menu bar, and select Settings. (The first time you access MultiOrder Shipping, the Getting Started dialog box is displayed. Click the Close button to close this dialog box.)

NOTE: At present, MultiOrder Shipping works only with U.S. Postal Service shipping. For other shipping services, use PayPal's manual shipping tool.

Figure 7.8
Configuring print settings.

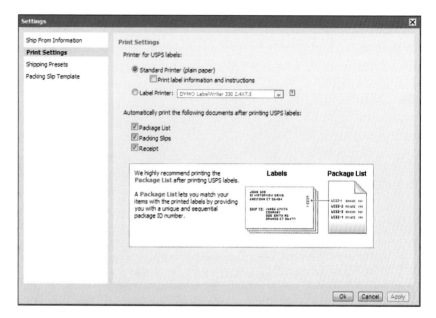

6. When the Settings dialog box appears, you will see four categories listed in the panel on the left. Select Ship From Information and choose the appropriate address. If you want your customers to receive a shipping notification via email, check the Send Email Notification to Recipient box.

7. Select Print Settings, shown in **Figure 7.8**, and choose a printer. You can also indicate whether you want to print accompanying package lists, packing slips, or receipts.

8. Select Shipping Presets and click Create. As you can see in **Figure 7.9**, this is how you quickly assign shipping details to a customer order. Give the preset a name, select the service type and package, choose a weight, decide if you want to provide shipping insurance, indicate whether you want to require signature confirmation, check if you want to hide the postage cost on the label, and then click the Save button.

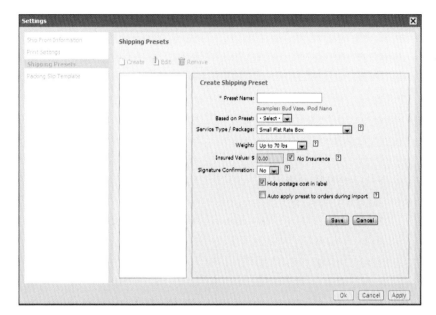

Figure 7.9
Creating shipping presets.

9. Repeat Step 8 to create additional shipping presets.

10. Select Packing Slip Template to customize the packing slip you include in your package. You can add your company logo and a message to the customer.

11. When you're done configuring these settings, click the OK button.

CREATING A BATCH SHIPPING ORDER

Once you have MultiOrder Shipping properly configured, you can start shipping. For each batch you ship, you need to import your recent PayPal orders and assign a shipping preset to each order. Follow these steps:

1. Open the MultiOrder Shipping tool.

2. Click the Import button on the toolbar, and then select PayPal Orders.

3. Click OK when your orders are finished importing.

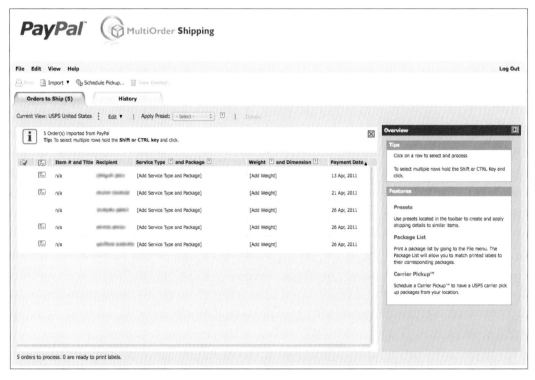

Figure 7.10 *Creating a batch shipping order.*

4. Make sure you have the Orders to Ship tab selected. You should see all your imported orders, as shown in **Figure 7.10**. Highlight an order to view the details for that order on the right side of the window.

5. Click one or more orders that will be using the same shipping preset. Hold down the Ctrl button on your keyboard to select multiple items (Command button on Mac).

6. Pull down the Apply Preset list and select the shipping preset. Information about the selected items is filled in automatically.

7. Repeat Steps 5 and 6 to apply presets to other orders.

8. To enter information about an order that doesn't fit any of your pre-sets, manually select Service Type, Package, Weight, and Dimension for that item.

9. When you're done applying presets and entering information, click the Print button on the toolbar to begin the printing process.

10. The Print Preview tab is now displayed. Verify that everything is cor-rect, and then click the Pay and Print button.

11. PayPal now contacts the U.S. Postal Service to obtain necessary infor-mation, and displays the standard Print dialog box. Select Print Labels, and then click the OK button to initiate batch printing.

PayPal now prints your labels and charges your account for the shipping fees incurred. Labels are printed in alphabetical order by last name.

Note that you can use the History tab to view past orders.

PayPal INSIDER

Tracking Shipments

Our most successful customers know they're not finished just because they've shipped an order. You need to be able to respond if a customer calls or emails to say he hasn't received his package.

This is a good reason to opt for delivery confirma-tion on every order you ship. Delivery confirmation lets you know that the package was delivered to a specific address on a specific date. You can go fur-ther and choose signature confirmation, but that incurs an additional cost and can be inconvenient for customers who are not at home to receive shipments. Delivery confirmation is simply a good investment.

We also recommend that you select the option to email customers when an item is shipped. This courtesy allows customers to know when the item is actually shipped, so they can estimate when it will arrive. Our customers have found that this cuts down on their support costs—think of it as proac-tive customer support.

Shipping Internationally

So far we've discussed using PayPal's shipping tools to ship domestically. PayPal also provides tools for international shipping.

In many ways, PayPal's international shipping tools are similar to its tools for domestic shipping. You select a shipping service, specify a shipping charge to the customer, and print a prepaid shipping label.

The big difference between international and domestic shipping is the need to fill out appropriate customs forms. While this is a somewhat tedious task, PayPal helps to automate the process.

CAUTION: Because of the higher incidence of fraud outside the U.S., international shipments do not qualify for PayPal's Seller Protection Policy.

Configuring International Shipping Settings

You configure PayPal's international shipping settings much the same way you configure domestic settings. From your profile, click My Selling Tools, and then, under the Shipping My Items heading, update your Shipping Calculations. When the next page appears, click the Start button in the Set Up International Shipping Methods section.

From here the set up should be familiar to you. Use the Shipping Region page to select the countries you ship to. Use the Shipping Method page to specify shipping methods and rates. Review and then save your settings.

Making an International Shipment

When shipping internationally, you have to ship manually, one order at a time, as batch shipping is only available for domestic orders. Go to your account overview or History page and click the Print Shipping Label button for the order you wish to ship.

The big difference here is that in addition to the prepaid shipping label, PayPal prints all necessary customs forms for shipping to the designated country. Just fill out the forms and have them available when you take the package to the post office for shipping.

NOTE: Depending on the type of item you're shipping and the weight of your package, you'll need either Form 2976 (green) or Form 2976-A (white). Customs forms aren't required on nonduty items that weigh less than 16 ounces.

The Bottom Line

PayPal helps to automate your shipping process from start to finish. You can configure your PayPal account to include various shipping methods and rates, and have those rates applied automatically during the checkout process. You can then use PayPal to print packing slips and shipping labels with prepaid postage, for both domestic and international shipments. MultiOrder Shipping even lets you batch together up to 50 different shipments, for faster processing and label printing. It's a complete shipping solution, all handled from within your PayPal account.

8

Managing Inventory

Inventory management is a challenge for retail businesses of all sizes. Whether you keep one or a thousand units of an item in stock, it's all too easy to deplete your inventory—and disappoint your customers. What you need is a way to keep track of what's in stock, so you know when to make or order more.

PayPal's Website Payments Standard offers just this kind of inventory management—adjusting inventory as sales are made—and much more, as you will see. After you read this chapter and spend some time setting up your configuration, you can start taking advantage of the robust inventory management features that PayPal has to offer.

Inventory Management with Website Payments Standard

Website Payments Standard packs a lot of features into its innocuous-looking payment buttons. You're familiar with how you can use the buttons to initiate sales from your website and have the transactions processed via the PayPal Shopping Cart. Now you'll learn that you can also configure them to keep track of your inventory levels: you enter how many units you start with initially, and it will track how many you've sold, and how many you have left.

PayPal can also notify you by email when your inventory levels run low (you specify the notification level), so you won't sell items that aren't in stock. This prevents erroneous transactions—and associated refunds—that result from selling merchandise that's not really available. You can even use Website Payments Standard to run regular inventory and sales reports, and help you identify sales patterns that affect your inventory management. It's all a matter of configuring your payment buttons with the proper information.

How Inventory Management Works

To use a payment button for inventory management, you need to configure certain settings for that button, and then save the button in your PayPal account setup. You can then track inventory levels for the item associated with that button. And if an item you sell has multiple options—color, size, and so forth—you can track inventory by each of these options. So if you're running low on a particular red sweater in XL, you'll know.

Even better, your customers will know. Instead of enabling customers to place orders for out-of-stock items, you can configure PayPal to notify them when an item is sold out. You can let a customer go ahead and place an order (creating a backorder for that item) or invite her to order another item, instead. If you wish, you can even transfer her to another URL (for a similar item, for example) when their original choice is out of stock.

Of course, PayPal will track your inventory levels for you and generate a helpful inventory report. You can also enable profit and loss tracking for each item in your inventory; PayPal not only tracks units sold, but also the gross profit generated for each item.

Inventory Management by Example

Let's look at how PayPal's inventory management works for a typical merchant.

For this example, consider a fictitious online merchant called the Super Big Shoestore, which sells shoes—and lots of them. Super Big uses PayPal's Website Payments Standard, and creates a Buy Now button for each SKU it carries.

Super Big receives a special shipment of 100 women's boots, in black. These boots cost $60 per pair, and Super Big sells them for $100. So Super Big generates a purchase button for these boots, and specifies the unit's cost, selling price, and initial inventory level. Super Big also specifies an alert point at the 30-unit level—that is, the retailer will be alerted when inventory drops to just 30 units in stock. That should provide enough lead time for Super Big to place a reorder with its supplier.

Super Big sells a lot of shoes, and this is a popular style; right out of the gate, they're selling five units per day of these black boots. With each order placed online, Super Big's inventory is automatically adjusted downward. At the end of the first day, Super Big's inventory is down to 95 units. After day two, inventory is 90 units. And so on.

Within 14 days, then, Super Big's inventory on this item is down to 30 units. While Super Big's inventory manager would have seen this when he accessed PayPal's inventory report, he doesn't read that report every day. Fortunately, PayPal generates an email alert and notifies Super Big that inventory on this SKU is now at the 30-unit level. The inventory manager receives this email and promptly places a new order with his supplier. The shipment arrives five days later, as expected, and Super Big never goes out of stock on this popular item.

NOTE: This example is admittedly simplified; a real-world shoe retailer probably would have carried that boot in several different colors and a variety of sizes. In that instance, the retailer would track sales and inventory for each specific variation.

This is quick and easy inventory management, and it's available to any merchant using PayPal's Website Payments Standard. It doesn't matter how many items you stock, how many units you keep in inventory, or even how many variations of a unit exist; PayPal keeps track of what's sold and what's on hand, automatically.

Configuring PayPal's Inventory Management— and Building Your Inventory

Inventory management in Website Payments Standard is activated when you create a Buy Now or Add to Cart button for a given item you're selling. The option to track inventory is available during the button creation process.

> **NOTE:** Learn more about creating payment buttons in Chapter 3, "Integrating PayPal with Your Site."

Let's return to the button-creation process discussed previously. In Step 1 on the Create PayPal Payment Button page, you determine what type of button to create, provide the item name and ID, specify the item price, and add shipping and tax details. This is also where you add a drop-down menu for various item options, such as size and color.

When you're using PayPal for inventory management, nothing changes in the Step 1 process—with one exception. While an item ID is optional with a normal payment button, this field is mandatory when you want to activate inventory management. So you must enter an identification number of some sort into the Item ID box, as shown in **Figure 8.1**.

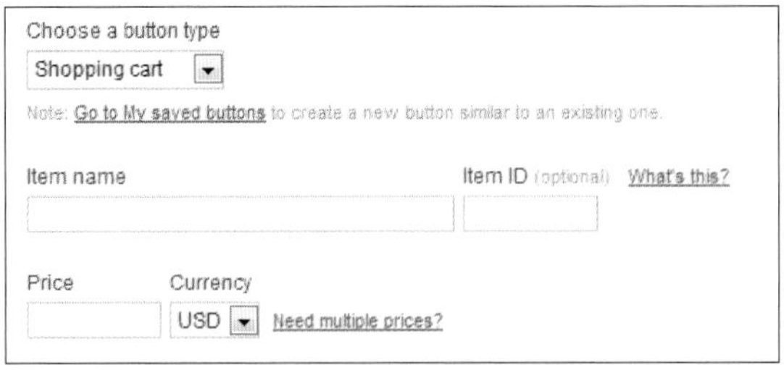

Figure 8.1

Enter a model or ID number into the Item ID box located in the Step 1 section.

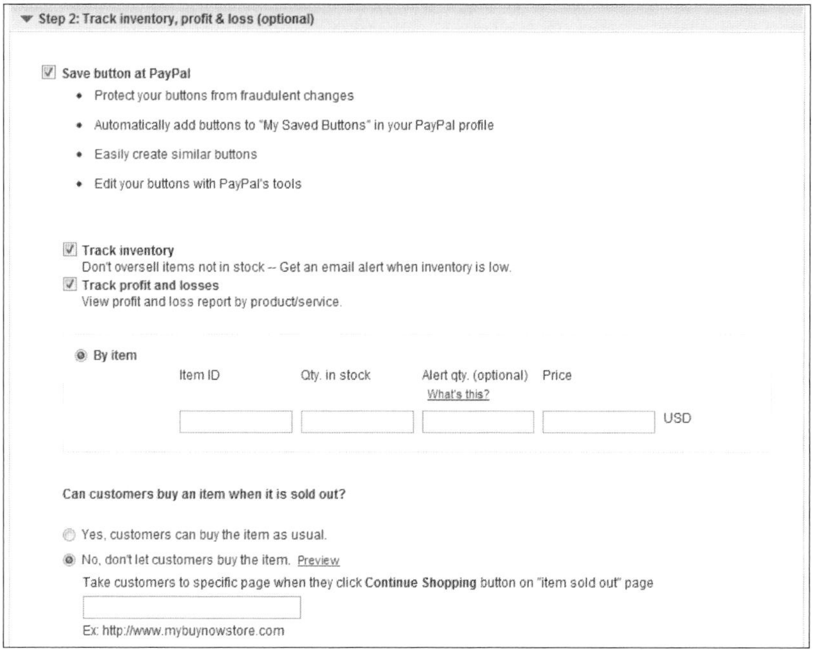

Figure 8.2
*Entering inventory
information in
Step 2.*

With Step 1 complete, you now proceed to and expand Step 2, shown in **Figure 8.2**. Let's walk through the specific steps you need to execute:

1. Check to Save the button at PayPal.

2. Check the Track inventory option.

3. If you want to include cost info to track this item's profit and loss, check that option.

4. Go to the By Item section. The Item ID should be prefilled, based on the entry you made in the Item ID field in Step 1. If not, enter the item number here.

5. Enter the number of units you currently have in stock into the Qty. in stock box.

6. If you want to be alerted when inventory reaches a reorder level, enter that level in the Alert qty. box. If you don't want a reorder alert, leave this box empty.

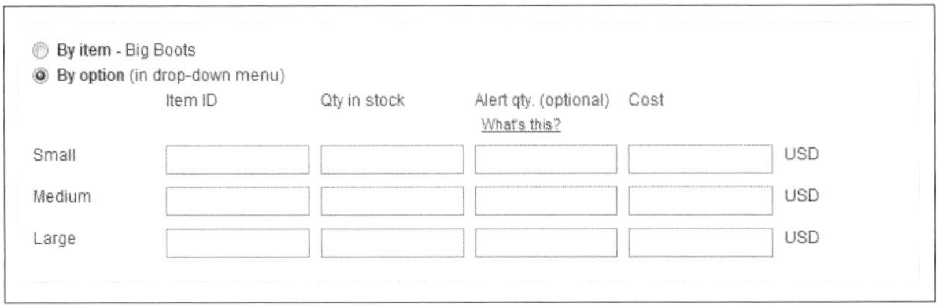

Figure 8.3

*Entering inventory
information for an
item with multiple
options.*

7. If you want to track profit and loss for this item, enter the item's unit cost in the Price box.

8. If you want customers to be able to order this item even when it's out of stock, select the "Yes, customers can buy the item as usual" option.

9. If you'd rather they not be able to order out-of-stock items, select the "No, don't let customers buy the item" option. You then enter the URL of a specific landing page on your site that customers will be directed to when they try to order a sold-out item. For example, you might construct a page that notes the specific item is currently not available but suggests another item to buy, instead.

10. Click the Create Button button to generate the button code.

As you can see, the process is actually fairly straightforward. It gets slightly more complex if you have an item with additional options, such as size or color. When you create a button for a multioption item, the Step 2 section changes to reflect this, as shown in **Figure 8.3**. Select "By option (in drop-down menu)" and you see a grid with rows for each available option—in our example, Small, Medium, and Large. Enter the item ID, quantity in stock, alert quantity, and cost information for each option, and then complete the rest of the process as normal.

NOTE: You can only track inventory against the options in one drop-down menu; you can't track options from two different drop-down menus. If you have more than one set of options, you'll need to break the second set of options into a separate payment button.

Monitoring the Customer Experience

When you add inventory management functionality to a payment button, it doesn't affect the customer experience at all—if the item is in stock. That is, the buyer clicks the Buy Now or Add to Cart button and the item is either purchased at that point or added to the shopping cart for future check out. All inventory information is passed to you, of course, but the customer doesn't see any of that; the inventory management happens behind the scenes.

If an item is out of stock, however, one of two things can happen.

If you opted to let the customer buy sold-out items, the purchase continues as normal. Obviously, the item doesn't ship, but you can then place the item on backorder for shipment when additional quantities arrive.

If you opted *not* to let the customer purchase sold-out items (this is the default, by the way), her experience is different. When she clicks the Buy Now or Add to Cart button, she's taken to the PayPal website, which displays a "Sorry, this item is sold out" error message. The customer then clicks the Continue Shopping button on that page to return to your website. She's returned to the page you specified when you created the button.

NOTE: If there is some quantity of the item in stock but not enough to fulfill the customer's complete order, PayPal displays a suggestion that the customer adjust her order to match the quantity on hand.

Tracking Reorders—and Replenishing Inventory

When you activate the inventory management functionality in Website Payments Standard, PayPal automatically tracks inventory levels with each customer purchase. A customer buys one unit of an item and your inventory level is automatically reduced by one unit. There's nothing you have to do in this regard.

This real-time tracking becomes more important when you specify a reorder level (alert quantity) when you create the payment button. As soon as the inventory level for an item reaches this level, PayPal sends you an email alerting you to this fact. You can then act on this alert accordingly, by placing a reorder with your supplier or otherwise replenishing stock. (Of course, you can also ignore the alert to let inventory levels run down on an older item you don't want to restock.)

If you do reorder the item, you then have to adjust your inventory levels when new quantities arrive. You do this by editing your saved button. Follow these steps:

1. Go to your profile, click My Selling Tools on the left, and then, under the Selling Online heading, click to update your PayPal buttons.

2. Select the button you wish to edit; the Qty Available and Price columns are now visible, as shown in **Figure 8.4**.

3. Click the Action drop-down menu for this item and select Edit Button.

Figure 8.4

Viewing your saved buttons.

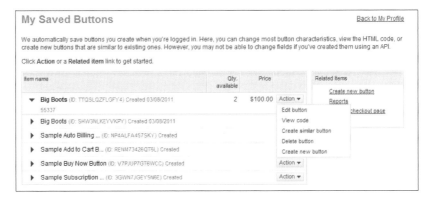

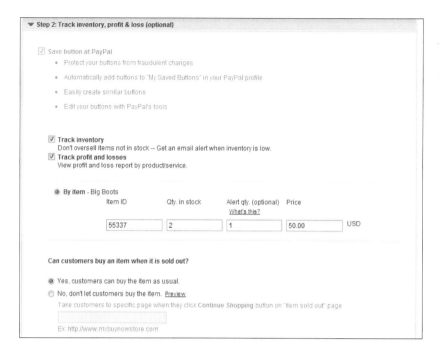

Figure 8.5
Editing a button's inventory information.

4. When the Edit your PayPal Payment Button page appears, scroll to and expand Step 2, shown in **Figure 8.5**.

5. Change the quantity in the Qty. in Stock box to reflect your new inventory level (that is, add the new units received to the existing units in the box).

6. If the new inventory was purchased at a different cost than the original inventory, enter that new cost into the Price box.

7. Click the Save Changes button.

PayPal now displays the code for the button, but you don't have to repaste it into your web page's underlying code; it's the same code as previously generated. What you've just done is update PayPal's system with your new inventory levels. Nothing needs to change on your website.

Running Inventory Reports

To better manage your inventory—and your business—you'll want to view data about the items you've sold and your stocking levels. You do this by displaying PayPal's Inventory and Profit & Loss Report, which you can access by selecting the My Account tab, and then clicking History > Reports. When the next page appears, click the Inventory and Profit & Loss Report link. When the next page appears, select a date range for the report, and then click the View Report button.

NOTE: You'll probably have to scroll the report to the right to see all available columns.

Figure 8.6

PayPal's Inventory and Profit & Loss Report.

As you can see in **Figure 8.6**, this report lists all the items for which you've created payment buttons. For each item, you see the following information:

- Button ID

- Item ID

- Item name

- Current inventory level (quantity currently in stock)

- Number of items sold (during the selected time period)

- Minimum selling price

- Maximum selling price

- Current price (the price specified on the button itself)

NOTE: Unless you've allowed discounts or sale pricing, the minimum and maximum selling prices will probably be the same.

- Cost price minimum (the minimum you paid per unit for inventory of this item)

- Cost price maximum (the maximum you paid per unit for inventory of this item)

- Discount amount (the total discount allowed from your stated item price—the total dollar amount generated from sales subtracted from the current price listed, for all items sold)

- PayPal fees (all transaction fees associated with sales of this item)

- Refunds (any refunds you've had to offer customers who returned this item)

- Shipping amount (total amount of shipping and handling fees paid)

- Tax amount (total amount of taxes collected on the items sold)

- Gross amount (the total dollar amount generated from sales plus the total of all shipping/handling fees)

- Profit (the total dollar amount generated from sales minus the total cost for all items sold)

- Profit margin (the dollar profit from the previous column divided by the total dollar amount generated from all items sold)

Naturally, totals for each column are displayed at the bottom of the report. To print the report, click the Print link above the report. To download a copy of the report in spreadsheet format, select Excel from the pull-down list above the report, and then click the Download button.

Inventory Management with Website Payments Pro

So far we've examined inventory management with Website Payments Standard. How, then, do you manage your inventory if you use Website Payments Pro instead?

The answer is, you manage your inventory using the same mechanisms you did before you signed in to PayPal. That's because Pro doesn't integrate directly with the items you have for sale on your website, as Standard does. Instead, Pro integrates with your shopping cart system. If you're using Pro, you're likely to have an existing inventory system and only rely on PayPal for some (or all) transaction processing. It's your shopping cart that manages your inventory (or interfaces with a separate inventory management or content management system), not PayPal.

If you're using a third-party shopping cart, it may *look* as if PayPal integrates with your inventory; that's a sign that the shopping cart provider did a good job designing things. (You want the entire process to appear as seamless as possible.) But all PayPal receives is data related to the customer's payment, not data related to what the customer is purchasing, so it can't track anything for you.

PayPal INSIDER

 ### Discovering Sales Patterns

The Inventory and Profit & Loss Report serves as a snapshot of where things stand for your business. You can get a picture of sales patterns over time by comparing reports from multiple months over time.

At PayPal, we've found that the easiest way to do this is to download consecutive monthly reports in Excel format. You can combine the monthly Excel data into a master spreadsheet, with different tabs for each month. This enables you to feed the summary data for each month into a separate tab and generate a graph. We suggest a simple line chart, which lets you view sales or inventory trends over time.

You may like the way we do our own PayPal reports, or you may want to view your data in a different way. We make it convenient for you to download the data in each report so that you can be as creative as your Excel skills allow.

The Bottom Line

PayPal offers detailed inventory and sales tracking for merchants using PayPal-hosted payment buttons, typically those signed up for Website Payments Standard. When you create a payment button, you specify the quantity on hand (and optionally the item cost); when a customer purchases that item by clicking the payment button, PayPal automatically adjusts the quantity on hand so you can re-order the item as needed. You can also configure PayPal to send an email alert when inventory drops to a specified level—ideal for restocking popular merchandise. You track your inventory levels via PayPal's Inventory and Profit & Loss Report, which also helps you track essential sales data for each item you carry, such as quantity sold, minimum/maximum selling price, and profit margin.

9
Making Payments

So far in this book we've addressed using PayPal to process online payments from your customers. But it goes both ways; you can also use PayPal to *make* payments to customers, suppliers, and your employees. It's a nice adjunct to PayPal's basic function of processing your incoming payment, and it can make your life easier.

Of course, you can transfer the funds in your PayPal account to your bank account and send payments to vendors the old-fashioned way. But once you have customer purchases building up a nice balance in your PayPal account, you might consider skipping those steps and simply sending payments directly from PayPal.

PayPal Payments: More than Payment Processing

PayPal facilitates all sorts of monetary transactions. Of course, PayPal handles payments from customers to retailers, either at the point of sale or when invoiced. PayPal also handles payments from eBay buyers to eBay sellers. People can also use PayPal to send money to other individuals—parents sending money to college kids, for example, or someone sending a monetary gift to a family member or friend.

More important to retailers, you can use PayPal to send money to individuals and other businesses. You can refund money to customers who've returned products or overpaid; you can pay your suppliers or contractors. You can even use PayPal to pay your own employees, in the form of one-time bonuses or ongoing salary. They're all just different types of online payments, after all.

PayPal's outgoing merchant payments are available to any business using PayPal, no matter which (if any) product you subscribe to. You don't need to use Website Payments Standard or Pro or any other business product to send money to another business or individual via PayPal. All you need is a PayPal account and some means of funding (typically your bank account, although you can also fund payments via credit card), and you're ready to go.

Issuing Customer Refunds

Let's start by examining how you can use PayPal to issue refunds to your customers. It's really quite easy.

Refunding Money from a PayPal Transaction

All of PayPal's order processing products have built-in refund functionality. You process refunds one at a time; in this scenario, a refund is linked to a specific sales transaction.

You can refund Completed, Pending, Cleared, or Uncleared payments; naturally, you can't refund payments that haven't been received. In addition, refunds issued against a specific transaction have to be made within 60 days of the original payment. (To issue refunds after 60 days, see the next section in this chapter.)

Here's how to issue a refund for any transaction processed by PayPal:

1. Log in to your PayPal account. If the transaction you are seeking does not appear in your Recent Activity click to see more transactions (or click the History tab).

2. When you see the transaction listed, look under the Order status/actions column. You should see either an Issue Refund button, or a drop down where that is one of the choices, as shown in **Figure 9.1**. Don't panic, choosing this does not send the refund yet!

> **NOTE:** If for some reason you do not see the option to issue a refund, click to see the transaction details and the "Issue a refund" link should appear there, if the transaction is eligible for a refund.

	Date		Type	Name/Email	Payment status	Details	Order status/Actions	Gross
☐	May 6, 2011		Payment To	GoDaddy.com, Inc.	Completed	Details		-$46.02 USD
☐	May 6, 2011		Payment From		Completed	Details	Issue refund	$20.00 USD
☐	May 6, 2011		Payment From		Completed	Details	Issue refund	$20.00 USD
☐	May 4, 2011		Payment From	Freshview Pty Ltd	Completed	Details		$2.94 USD
☐	May 4, 2011		Payment From		Completed	Details	Print shipping label ▾	$30.00 USD
☐	May 3, 2011		Payment From		Completed	Details	Add Tracking Info / Mark as shipped	$30.00 USD
☐	May 3, 2011		Payment From		Cleared	Details	Issue Refund	$30.00 USD

Figure 9.1

Initiating a customer refund from the Activity or History list.

Figure 9.2 *Enter details of a customer refund.*

3. When the transaction details page appears, click the link under the transaction amount: Issue a refund.

4. When the Issue Refund page appears, as shown in **Figure 9.2**, enter the amount of the refund. Click Continue.

5. Review the refund details, then click the Issue Refund button—this actually sends the refund.

You can issue either a full or partial refund. For most commercial transactions you're not limited to refunding the entire amount of the transaction, but for pending (or personal) transactions you can only refund the full amount.

When you issue a full refund, PayPal credits back to you the original transaction fee paid, minus a 30-cent processing fee. When you issue a partial refund, PayPal credits back to you a portion of the original transaction fee.

Making Payments to Vendors

You can use PayPal send money to your vendors to pay open invoices. The recipient does not need to have a PayPal account. The one caveat for using PayPal to pay vendors is that the vendor will have to pay a nominal transaction fee to retrieve the funds. In this instance, your vendor functions as any PayPal seller, and is charged accordingly.

Here's how to do it:

CAUTION: Make sure your vendor accepts PayPal payments—and is willing to pay the corresponding transaction fee—before you send the payment.

1. Log in to your PayPal account and select the Send Money tab.

2. When the Send Money page appears, enter the recipient's email address into the To box.

3. Enter the amount you're paying into the Amount box; make sure USD is selected in the associated pull-down list. (If you're sending funds in a different currency, select that currency instead.)

4. Select the Purchase tab, as shown in **Figure 9.3**.

5. Assuming that you're paying for goods delivered from a vendor, select the Goods option.

6. Click the Continue button.

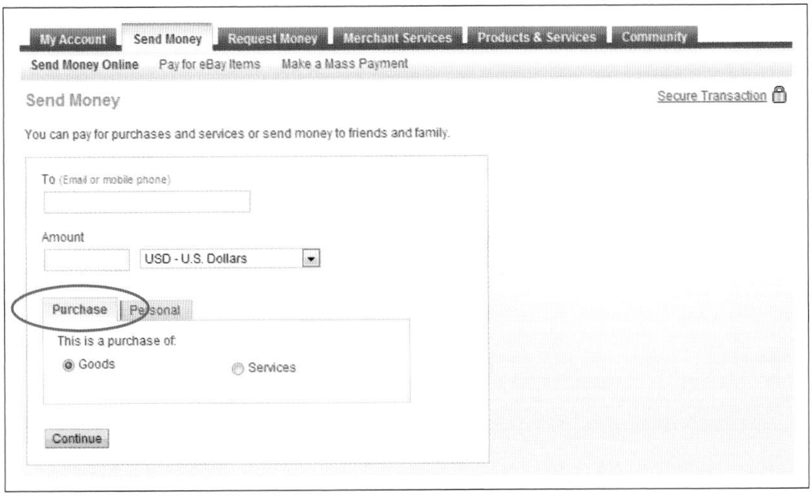

Figure 9.3
Sending a payment to a vendor for goods received.

7. PayPal now displays the Review your payment and send page. Review the details of the payment, then confirm or change the payment method.

8. Enter the subject of the email in the Subject box.

9. Enter your own message (such as the invoice number you're paying) in the Message box.

10. Click the Send Money button.

The vendor receives email notification of the payment and can access those funds from their PayPal account.

Making Payments to Contractors and Employees

You can use PayPal to pay contractors and freelancers under your employ, as well as your regular employees. The process is similar to that used to pay vendors. Note, however, that any contractor or employee you pay must have a PayPal account, and will be liable for the corresponding transaction fees.

PayPal INSIDER

 ### PayPal for Payroll Processing?

Paying employees via PayPal does not involve traditional paper checks; employees access funds paid online via their PayPal accounts. This eliminates the printing and distributing of checks, and saves employees a trip to the bank.

Be aware, however, that this solution may not be universally embraced by employees who are used to receiving a physical paycheck each week. Each employee must have a PayPal account, as well as access to a computer and the Internet. In addition, you may need to set up training sessions.

From the employer's perspective, be aware that payroll processing at PayPal is not a comprehensive accounting product. You need to do your own payroll calculations and store that information offline.

If you are an employer who uses 1099 contractors, rather than payroll employees, PayPal might be more attractive to you—especially if the contractors are scattered around the country or the world.

Here's what to do:

1. Log in to your PayPal account and select the Send Money tab.

2. When the Send Money page appears, enter the recipient's email address into the To box.

TIP: As contractors and employees may not be accustomed to having processing fees being taken out of their paychecks, you may want to increase the amount paid to cover the fees.

3. Enter the amount you're paying into the Amount box; make sure USD is selected in the associated pull-down list. (If you're sending funds in a different currency, select that currency instead.)

4. Select the Purchase tab.

5. Select the Services option.

6. Click the Continue button.

7. PayPal now displays the Review your payment and send page. Review the details of the payment, then confirm or change the payment method.

8. Enter the subject of the email in the Subject box.

9. Enter your own custom message (such as the job or invoice number for the contractor or freelancer) in the Message box.

10. Click the Send Money button.

The recipient receives notification of the payment and can access those funds from her PayPal account.

Using PayPal's Mass Payment

So far we've discussed single payments to individuals and businesses. This approach is fine if you make only occasional payments of this type, but it can be cumbersome if your payment load increases.

If you make a lot of payments via PayPal, consider using PayPal's Mass Payment option. This product enables any entity with a Premier or Business account to send payments to multiple recipients with relative ease.

When to Use Mass Payment

When might you use PayPal's Mass Payment? Here's a short list:

- Affiliate commissions
- Customer rebates
- Pay-to-surf rewards
- Employee benefits/bonuses
- Lottery prizes
- Survey incentives

And, of course, to handle your entire employee payroll.

NOTE: Individual payments to recipients cannot exceed $10,000 U.S. (Limits vary from country to country.)

Paying for Mass Payments

Mass Payment itself is free, and available to all businesses using PayPal. You pay for each payment processed—that is, for each payment to an individual. Your fee is 2% of the payment amount, up to a maximum of $1.00 US per payment.

Funding a Mass Payment

Unlike other forms of payments, a Mass Payment can only be funded from money transferred from your bank account to your PayPal account. You cannot use credit cards to fund Mass Payments.

Creating a Mass Payment File

Before you create a Mass Payment, you need to collect some basic information—in particular, the payees' email addresses and payment amounts. That's actually less than you need to process a conventional check payment, where you typically need the payee's street address, too.

Next, you need to create a Mass Payment file. This is a tab-delimited text file that contains a list of all the people you're paying and how much you're paying them.

You can easily create this file in Microsoft Excel. Just open a new spreadsheet with three columns (and optional fourth and fifth columns), as follows:

- Column 1 should contain the payees' email addresses, one per row.

- Column 2 should contain the payment amount for each payee.

- Column 3 should contain a three-letter code for the currency in which the payments will be made. The three-letter code for U.S. dollars is USD; you can find codes for other currencies on the PayPal website.

> **NOTE:** Each Mass Payment file can contain payments in only one currency. To make payments in different currencies, you must create separate Mass Payment files.

- Column 4 (optional) can contain recipient IDs you can use to track and reconcile payments. Each ID must be no more than 30 characters long, and cannot contain any spaces.

- Column 5 (also optional) can contain a customized note to each recipient. (The note will be inserted into the email notice of payment.)

Figure 9.4 shows what a typical Mass Payment file might look like.

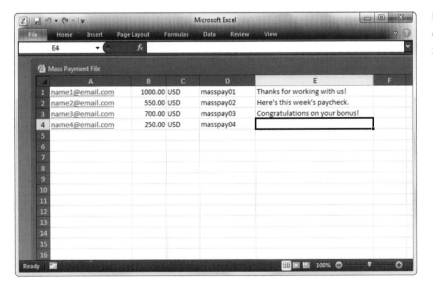

Figure 9.4

Creating a Mass Payment file in Excel.

Once created, you should save the Excel file as a Text (Tab delimited) file. Now you're ready to upload the file and send the Mass Payment.

NOTE: You can include up to 5,000 individual payments in a single Mass Payment file.

Sending a Mass Payment

Once you've created your Mass Payment file, follow these steps to send the payments:

1. Log in to your PayPal account and select the Send Money tab.

2. Select the Make a Mass Payment subtab.

3. When the Mass Payment page appears, as shown in **Figure 9.5**, click the Upload button. When the Open dialog box appears, navigate to and select your Mass Payment file, then click the Open button.

4. Pull down the My payment recipients are identified by list and select Email address.

Figure 9.5

Sending a Mass Payment.

5. Enter a subject for the emails you'll send in the Email subject box.

6. Enter a customized message to your payees in the Message to recipient box.

7. Click the Review button.

8. Review the information on the next page, then click the Submit button.

Receiving Funds

Once you send the Mass Payment, PayPal automatically transfers funds from your account to the accounts of all your payees. PayPal also sends email messages to the payees, notifying them that they've been paid.

TIP: You should notify each payee in advance that you're sending payment via PayPal, and that they'll each need a PayPal account to accept payment.

If the payee already has a PayPal account, and the email the payment was sent to is confirmed, the money automatically shows up in the payee's bank account. If the payee doesn't have a PayPal account, or has not yet confirmed her email address, then she needs to click the link in the payment notification email and complete the account setup and receive the funds.

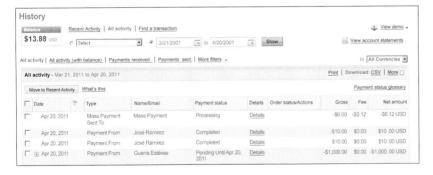

Figure 9.6
Viewing Mass Payment transactions.

Record Keeping

PayPal tracks all the payments you make on your History page, as shown in **Figure 9.6**. You can see which payments have been accepted and which are yet unclaimed, and reconcile your account accordingly.

TIP: It's also possible to send mass payments using your own internal payment system, via the PayPal MassPay API. Go to www.x.com/community/ppx/mass_pay for more details and programming assistance.

The Bottom Line

PayPal can be used for all manner of outgoing payments. You can issue full or partial refunds for any PayPal-based transaction. You can also use PayPal to pay vendors, contractors, and employees on an individual basis. PayPal also offers Mass Payment, which enables you to process multiple payments—such as large payroll transactions—via a single uploadable file.

10

Avoiding Fraudulent Transactions

Fraudulent transactions affect your bottom line. Getting scammed online has the same effect as shoplifting does in a brick-and-mortar store; it's a loss, pure and simple. When you're the victim of a fraudulent transaction, that's money out of your pocket—you're on the hook for all losses.

To protect your profit margin, it's imperative that you protect your business from fraudulent transactions. That's where working with PayPal is a good idea; PayPal offers a variety of anti-fraud programs and services that help to minimize the effects of online scammers.

Understanding Fraudulent Transactions

There are many ways a seller can be scammed online. And don't kid yourself—online fraud for merchants is just as big a problem as the various forms of online fraud that plague consumers.

Effects of Online Fraud

The most obvious effect is that you have paid out money for a transaction that is not legitimate. In addition, some credit card processors charge penalties to merchants that are the victim of credit card fraud—anywhere from $15 to $30 per fraudulent transaction. That's painful.

Online fraud has been decreasing, but it's still a major problem. According to the CyberSource 12th Annual Online Fraud Report, fraudulent orders accounted for 0.9% of all online orders in 2010. (That's beyond the 2.7% of orders that merchants declined on suspicion of fraud.) That adds up to a total yearly loss of $2.7 billion.

According to CyberSource, about half of these losses come in the form of chargebacks; the rest come from credits issued in response to fraud complaints. That means you can't judge your own fraud-related losses by chargebacks alone—they're only half the story.

Types of Online Fraud

How can your business become an unwitting victim of online fraud? There are, unfortunately, several different ways that dishonest users can scam you online. Here are a few of the possible situations that an online merchant might encounter:

- **The buyer claims not to receive an item**. A customer purchases an item from you. You ship it to the customer. The customer then claims that he never received the item and asks for a refund. If you refund the money, you're out the cost of the item plus the purchase price—and the scammer has a brand new item obtained at no cost.

- **The buyer claims an item is not as described**. This is a similar scam to the "item not received" scam. The customer purchases an item from you, you ship the item, and then the customer claims that the item isn't what was described. It's used instead of new, the wrong size, doesn't have the features promised, or otherwise not what she ordered. To pacify the customer you issue a full or partial refund, which puts you out the cost of the original item plus the cost of the refund. The scammer, of course, has a nice new product at no cost or at a reduced price.

- **The buyer claims an item was damaged in shipment**. This is a variation of the "not as described" scam. You ship to the customer the item purchased, and then the customer claims that the item was damaged in transit. Rather than dealing with the shipping service, you issue a full or partial refund. (Or maybe you issue a refund in advance, anticipating settlement from the shipping service.) The scammer gets an undamaged item at a substantial discount.

- **The buyer pays with a stolen credit card or a hijacked bank account**. The previous scams are all pretty much one-time affairs. (Although a lot of these single issues can add up to a large number.) A much more damaging form of fraud comes from professional identity theft, where a criminal steals a customer's credit card or debit card, or somehow hijacks the customer's bank account. The criminal then uses the stolen data or information to make one or more purchases, typically large ones, from you (and presumably other merchants). It looks like a standard transaction from your end and you ship the merchandise— typically to a fake address (known as a *freight forwarder*) set up just for the purpose of receiving illegally obtained merchandise. (The merchandise is then typically fenced or resold by other criminal rings.) When the original consumer—the one who was ripped off—notices the fraudulent account activity and makes a formal complaint, the consumer's credit card company or bank initiates a chargeback *against you* to recover the consumer's funds. This activity typically results in you being out the cost of the fraudulently obtained merchandise, and having the sales price for said items deducted from your credit account.

  > **CAUTION:** Most credit processing agreements hold online merchants liable for any losses incurred from fraudulent credit card payments.

- **Identity theft**. Identity (ID) theft isn't just for individuals. Many businesses find that criminals somehow obtain usernames, passwords, and other information that lets them either hack into their accounts or systems or make purchases while pretending to be someone authorized by your business. In the best-case scenario (and it's not so good), the thieves order various items and you pay for them. In the worst-case scenario, the criminals hack into your internal systems and wreak havoc, up to and including stealing your customers' personal data and shutting down your systems and servers. It's not something you want to happen.

NOTE: Don't confuse legitimate customer complaints with purposeful fraudulent behavior. A genuine issue concerning the receipt of an item, for example, is different from a scammer who falsely claims not to have received an item in an effort to defraud you.

How Criminals Obtain Fraudulent Information

As you can see, the most damaging forms of online fraud involve some form of ID theft—either of your ID or your customers' IDs. How, exactly, do criminals obtain this information?

When it comes to identity theft, know that it's not exclusively an online activity. Thieves have been appropriating confidential information since the first information was classified as confidential, and the vast majority of identity theft still takes place outside the online world.

That said, there are lots of different ways a criminal can get you or your customers' confidential information. Here are some of them:

- Steal a person's wallet or purse.

- Steal a company's or individual's postal mail, especially bank and credit card statements, as well as preapproved credit card offers that arrive in the post, unsolicited.

- Complete a change of address form with the U.S. Postal Service to divert a person's mail to another location.

- Rummage through a company's or an individual's trash (sometimes called "dumpster diving").

- Fraudulently obtain an individual's or a company's credit report by posing as a landlord or employer.

- Talk a company's human resources department into providing a person's personnel records.

- Buy personal or company information from inside sources, typically store or company employees.

- Use "packet sniffer" software to obtain passwords and numbers while users are online.

- Purchase or otherwise obtain illegally gathered information from an underground website or Internet Relay Chat (IRC) channel in what is known as the Dark Web.

- Use social engineering and phishing techniques to con people into providing confidential information via phone, email, instant messaging, or social networking sites.

- Intercept confidential information transmitted across nonsecure wired and wireless networks.

In short, there are lots of different ways that confidential information can be stolen. And once stolen, that information can be used to commit fraud against your business.

Reducing Online Fraud

However it comes, most merchants can't afford the financial loss caused by fraudulent transactions. You need to take aggressive steps to cut down on your fraud potential—and PayPal can help. Here are some of the things you can do:

- **Ship only to confirmed addresses**. Criminals who hijack consumers' accounts typically ship the illicit merchandise to some other address—not to the original consumer. For that reason, you need to be on the lookout for address inconsistencies, especially orders that have you sending the merchandise to an address other than that originally recorded for a customer. Especially suspicious are orders that have a billing address in one country and a shipping address in another.

- **Track all packages**. This is a great way to protect against fraudsters who claim not to receive a package. Get shipping or delivery confirmation so you have a good defense against this type of scam.

- **Insure all packages**. Protect yourself against claims of shipping damage by purchasing insurance for all the items you ship. This way you're protected if an item actually does get lost or damaged in shipment—or if a recipient claims the package was never delivered or arrived damaged.

- **Beware unusual customer requests**. The criminal element typically operates outside the norm. As such, you should beware of any suspicious requests on an order, such as customers willing to pay any price for rush delivery, split payments made from different PayPal accounts or credit cards, payments sent piecemeal from the same PayPal account, and orders that are not paid for in a single, full payment. You should also be suspicious of orders—especially from new customers—that are substantially larger than your typical order, or are for multiple items of the same style, color, or size. All of these are red flags that something foul may be afoot.

- **Check out your buyers**. You also need to know who you're selling to. Make sure that new customers have a verified PayPal account and a confirmed address before you ship.

What do you do if you receive a suspicious order online? A good first step is to call the customer to confirm. You should also take advantage of PayPal's various anti-fraud services, which we'll discuss next.

Using PayPal's Anti-fraud Services

PayPal offers a variety of services and technologies designed to help identify and prevent fraudulent transactions. In particular, PayPal has a team of more than 2,000 fraud-fighting specialists working 24/7 on your behalf, as well as highly effective anti-fraud risk models and detection techniques that help stop fraud in its tracks.

Fighting Fraud Online

What measures does PayPal take to help reduce fraud? There are many, and they include the following:

- Address confirmation to protect against packages being shipped to places other than the legitimate customer's residence.

NOTE: PayPal verifies the customer's credit card billing address; shipping to an address other than this confirmed address is not advised.

- Industry-leading data encryption, to keep hackers from stealing transmitted data—and keep merchant transactions and financial information private.

- Integrated shipping and package tracking, so you know that your packages get where they're supposed to go.

- Transaction screening to alert merchants to suspicious account activity. PayPal uses highly sophisticated fraud models to identify potentially fraudulent transactions before they're completed.

- Industry-standard Address Verification Service (AVS) and Credit Card Verification Value (CVV2) checks as additional layers of protection against identity theft.

- Dispute resolution assistance, even for low-volume sellers, through the PayPal Resolution Center. PayPal aims for fair and speedy resolution for any dispute that should occur between buyers and sellers. This helps to ward off unwarranted refunds and chargebacks—often before they reach the chargeback level.

- A full-time chargeback fighting team, focused on denying fraudulent chargebacks from unscrupulous buyers.

PayPal's Anti-fraud Team

In addition to various anti-fraud tools and technologies, PayPal offers highly trained security teams that help to keep your sensitive data private, and your transactions clean. These professionals work behind the scenes, monitoring activity and possible fraud indicators to ensure a safer network.

PayPal's anti-fraud team employs a combination of sophisticated risk models and advanced technology to detect and often predict suspicious activity and help eliminate identity theft. The company's fraud experts also work closely with the FBI and other law enforcement agencies to identify and combat fraud wherever it occurs. PayPal's team is charged with making every PayPal transaction as safe and as seamless as possible—for all parties.

Should PayPal's fraud experts identify suspicious activity regarding one of your transactions, the transaction is placed on hold for 24 hours while the risk team determines its validity. PayPal will also alert you by email or have a representative call you, so you can then take whatever action is appropriate.

Employing Fraud Management Filters

If you use one of PayPal's payment processing products, you're protected by multiple Fraud Management Filters. These are tools that can identify payment characteristics that may indicate fraudulent activity.

If a transaction is flagged by one of these filters, you then have the option of denying payments that are likely to result in fraudulent transactions, or of accepting payments that are not typically a problem. You can even opt to further investigate flagged transactions, by comparing prior orders, for example, or by contacting the customer for more information.

Who Can Use Fraud Management Filters

PayPal provides free filters for all business accounts. These basic filters screen against the country of origin, the value of transactions, and such, thus protecting you from obvious fraudulent activity.

When you subscribe to Website Payments Pro, you have access to more advanced filters (at an additional charge). These filters screen against credit card and address information, lists of high-risk indicators, and additional transaction characteristics.

Benefits of Using Fraud Management Filters

There are several benefits of using PayPal's Fraud Management Filters. In particular, you save valuable time by letting PayPal review transactions instead of doing it yourself. You also save money by identifying and stopping potentially risky transactions; this reduces chargebacks and lowers your cost of doing business. Finally, you typically end up with more accepted payments, because PayPal applies your rules evenly, and with greater accuracy; good customers are less often rejected falsely.

How Fraud Management Filters Work

Figure 10.1 shows how a Fraud Management Filter works. In essence, there are three steps involved:

1. You configure your specific Fraud Management Filters to either flag or hold for review suspicious transactions, or to deny riskier payments.

2. Based on the settings you specify, your filters review all incoming payments.

3. Your filters automatically flag, hold for review, or deny payments.

As an example, consider the Maximum Transaction Amount Filter. Let's say you set up a $200 maximum transaction amount; any orders over this level are flagged for review. When a criminal using a stolen ID tries to place an order for $500, the order is flagged and you take the step of calling the customer to confirm the order. When the legitimate individual answers the phone, you (both) discover the attempted criminal activity.

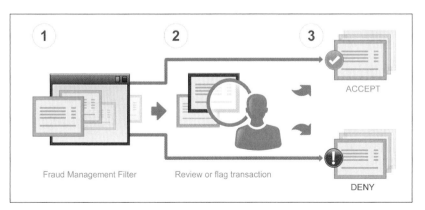

Figure 10.1
The three steps involved with a Fraud Management Filter.

You deny the fraudulent transaction, and the victim of identity theft takes action to stop further purchases on the stolen credit card.

In reality, most payments are accepted by the filters, as they do not show the characteristics you designated and thus do not indicate fraud. Those payments that are potentially fraudulent, however, are stopped and dealt with in the method you specified.

Selecting Fraud Management Filters

What Fraud Protection Filters are offered? It depends on which PayPal product you use.

> **NOTE:** If you use a third-party shopping cart provider, consult with your vendor to see which PayPal Fraud Management Filters are supported.

All PayPal business users have access to the following three basic filters:

- **Country Monitor Filter**, which identifies transactions based on the country of origin.

- **Maximum Transaction Amount Filter**, which identifies transactions that exceed a specified value.

- **Unconfirmed Address Filter**, which screens for payments above a specified amount when the shipping address entered by the customer has not yet been confirmed by PayPal.

Website Payments Pro subscribers have access to the following advanced filters, at an additional cost:

- **Address Verification Partial Match Filter**, which screens for transactions where the billing address entered by the customer doesn't completely match the information maintained by the card issuer.

- **Address Verification Service No Match Filter**, which screens for transactions where the billing address entered by the customer doesn't match the information provided by the card issuer.

- **Address Verification Service Unavailable or Not Supported Filter**, which screens for instances where the Address Verification Service (AVS) is unable to verify the billing address.

- **Bank Identification Number Filter**, which screens for payments from credit cards with Bank Identification Numbers (BINs) that have historically been associated with a high rate of fraudulent transactions. BINs, which identify the bank issuing the card, are checked against a "Risk List" maintained by PayPal.

- **Billing/Shipping Address Mismatch Filter**, which screens for payments with different billing and shipping addresses.

- **Card Security Code Mismatch Filter**, which identifies transactions with differences in the credit card security code.

- **Email Address Domain Filter**, which screens for email addresses with historically high rates of fraud, using a "Risk List" of email domains maintained by PayPal.

- **IP Address Range Filter**, which screens for payments from Internet Protocol (IP) addresses that have historically high instances of fraud, using a "Risk List" maintained by PayPal.

- **IP Address Velocity Filter**, which screens for multiple payments made from the same IP address.

- **Large Order Number Filter**, which screens for transactions based on the number of items purchased, looking for larger-than-normal quantities.

- **PayPal Fraud Model Filter**, which screens for payments that would have been declined by PayPal's fraud model.

- **Suspected Freight Forwarder Filter**, which screens for payments where the shipping address is a known freight forwarder, using a "Risk List" of U.S. shipping addresses maintained by PayPal.

- **Total Purchase Price Minimum Filter**, which identifies transactions that are less than a specified amount.

- **Zip Code Filter**, which screens for billing addresses that have historically high rates of fraud using a "Risk List" of U.S. shipping addresses maintained by PayPal.

> **NOTE:** Available filters are determined by agreement between you and PayPal; not all merchants are granted access to all filters.

Understanding Filter Settings

You can configure each individual Fraud Management Filter to automatically accept or deny a transaction, or to review or flag a transaction. **Table 10.1** details each of these settings.

Table 10.1 **Fraud Management Filter Settings**

Setting	Description
Accept	Accepts the payment. This setting is used only by the Total Purchase Price Minimum filter, which causes PayPal to accept transactions that fall below a minimum transaction amount.
Deny	Denies the payment. Use this setting only if you're positive you want the associated filter to automatically disqualify the payment. For example, you might use this setting to deny payments from countries with which it's too risky or difficult to conduct business.
Review	Makes the payment pending your review. Use this setting when you want to evaluate the transaction and then make a case-by-case decision on whether to accept or deny the payment.
Flag	Accepts the payment but flags it for later evaluation. This is a good setting to use when first testing the effect of a filter, or when you're not sure you want to review the payment but want an easy way to locate the flagged payment should you decide to look at it.

Activating Fraud Management Filters

PayPal's Fraud Management Filters are not activated by default. You must configure the filters you want before they can take effect.

To activate and configure Fraud Management Filters, follow these steps:

1. Go to your profile, click My Selling Tools on the left, and locate the heading: Getting Paid and Managing My Risk. Under this you will see that you can update your settings for Managing Risk and Fraud.

NOTE: You can activate multiple Fraud Management Filters; you're not limited to using just one at a time.

2. When the Edit My Filter Settings page appears, as shown in **Figure 10.2**, check those filters you want to use. The first time you do this, you will be asked to agree to the terms of Terms of Service for Fraud Management Filters.

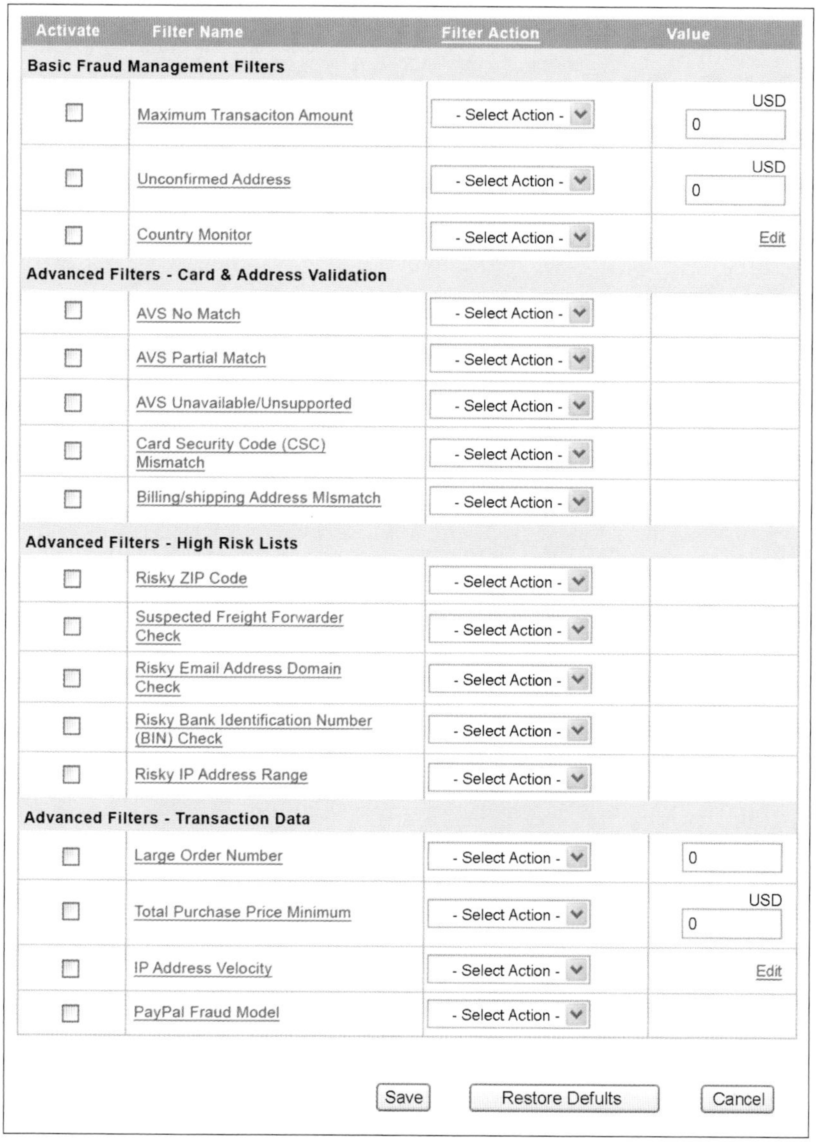

Activate	Filter Name	Filter Action	Value
Basic Fraud Management Filters			
☐	Maximum Transaciton Amount	- Select Action - ▾	USD 0
☐	Unconfirmed Address	- Select Action - ▾	USD 0
☐	Country Monitor	- Select Action - ▾	Edit
Advanced Filters - Card & Address Validation			
☐	AVS No Match	- Select Action - ▾	
☐	AVS Partial Match	- Select Action - ▾	
☐	AVS Unavailable/Unsupported	- Select Action - ▾	
☐	Card Security Code (CSC) Mismatch	- Select Action - ▾	
☐	Billing/shipping Address MIsmatch	- Select Action - ▾	
Advanced Filters - High Risk Lists			
☐	Risky ZIP Code	- Select Action - ▾	
☐	Suspected Freight Forwarder Check	- Select Action - ▾	
☐	Risky Email Address Domain Check	- Select Action - ▾	
☐	Risky Bank Identification Number (BIN) Check	- Select Action - ▾	
☐	Risky IP Address Range	- Select Action - ▾	
Advanced Filters - Transaction Data			
☐	Large Order Number	- Select Action - ▾	0
☐	Total Purchase Price Minimum	- Select Action - ▾	USD 0
☐	IP Address Velocity	- Select Action - ▾	Edit
☐	PayPal Fraud Model	- Select Action - ▾	

[Save]   [Restore Defults]   [Cancel]

Figure 10.2
Activating Fraud Management Filters on the Edit My Filter Settings page.

3. For each filter selected, pull down the corresponding Filter Action list and select an action for that filter.

4. When a filter should be triggered by an associated value, enter that amount into the Value box.

5. When done, click the Save button.

Reporting Fraud

How do you let PayPal know about potential fraud? It's important for businesses to report any suspected instances of fraud, no matter how small. Not only does this protect you, it also helps to protect other businesses that might fall victim to possible fraud.

Reporting Unauthorized Activity on Your PayPal Account

If you notice unauthorized account activity, this may mean that someone has hacked into your PayPal account. You should report this immediately via the Resolution Center.

After you log in to your PayPal account and open the Resolution Center, click the Dispute a Transaction link, the select Unauthorized Transaction. Click the Continue button and follow the onscreen instructions to report the issue.

Reporting Unauthorized Activity on Your PayPal Debit Card

If you have a PayPal debit card and notice unauthorized transactions, you should immediately call the number listed on the back of the card. Alternatively, you can email PayPal at the address listed on the back of the card. In either instance, be prepared to provide details about the transactions in question.

Reporting Fake (Phishing) Emails and Websites

If you receive a questionable email purporting to be from PayPal, or if you're directed to an official-looking PayPal website that doesn't have the proper www.paypal.com address, chances are you're in the middle of a phishing scam. Not only should you *not* click any links in the email or on the website, but you should also report the issue to PayPal. The best way to do this is to forward the fake email to spoof@paypal.com. Likewise, you can send an email to that address containing the URL of the spoof website.

NOTE: All emails from PayPal address you by first and last name; if it says "Dear PayPal Member," it's probably not legitimate.